SUCCESS TALK

D1491275

Other Books by James Humes

INSTANT ELOQUENCE

PODIUM HUMOR

RULES SPEAKERS PLAY

SPEAKER'S TREASURY OF ANECDOTES
ABOUT THE FAMOUS

HOW TO GET INVITED TO THE WHITE HOUSE

CHURCHILL: SPEAKER OF THE CENTURY

TALK YOUR WAY TO THE TOP

HOW TO MAKE THE BEST PRESENTATION
OF YOUR LIFE

SUCCESS TALK

How to Be an Effective Speaker and Communicator

James C. Humes

NewsMax.com

West Palm Beach, Florida

SECOND EDITION

Copy Editor: Rita Samols
Designer: Becky Mangus
Index by Alberta M. Morrison

Library of Congress Cataloging-in-Publication Data
Humes, James C.
    Success Talk
    Includes index.
    1. Public speaking.   I. Title
PN4021.H86   1988   808.5'1   87-45058
87-45058
ISBN 0-9716807-6-0
03 04 05 06 07 SC 10 9 8 7 6 5 4 3 2 1

Contents

CONTENTS

The three most difficult things for a man to do are to climb a wall leaning towards you, to kiss a girl leaning away from you, and to make an after-dinner speech.

—WINSTON CHURCHILL

Introduction

Speaking Is Leadership

Next to the White House stands a French Renaissance mausoleum called the Executive Office Building, where most of the White House staff work. On the third floor of the EOB is a small auditorium. There in December 1983 for two days, President Reagan, Vice President Bush, Cabinet members, and key White House aides outlined and explained their policies to a group of financial contributors.

I spoke too, on the subject of public speaking. And while I was arguably least in prominence or qualifications, I was also the only one to be awarded a standing ovation. Hardly anyone in that audience had heard of James C. Humes, yet I was able to bring them to their feet when others, including the Great Communicator himself, Ronald Reagan, did not. Why was that? Well, first, because I planned for that kind of response. As a professional speaker and as one who would be introduced as communications expert, I had to be inspiring. Why should an audience take to heart a message about speaking from someone who was a dull speaker?

Obviously if the President, who is a superb speaker, had wanted to be eloquent, he could have been. To him it was just another appearance in a day crowded with engagements. Similarly, most of the other Cabinet members viewed their invitation as a chore in a busy day.

A month later I had a call at my Philadelphia home from one of the listeners. He asked if he could meet me. I readily agreed. Over lunch the visitor, who was a corporation executive, sounded me out on the political situation. We talked amiably. He had obviously retained some of the key ideas I had proposed in my speech, and he questioned me about them.

At the end of the lunch, I almost dropped my coffee cup when he asked me, "Have you considered running for President yourself? A group of us who heard you think you have that communicating ability that spells leadership."

I replied, "I love my country; in fact, I love it so much that I would never inflict myself upon it!"

I tell this story with some embarrassment because I don't want any of my friends who might read this account to think that I suffer from delusions of grandeur. Yet the crazy, improbable tale does prove a couple of points. First, really good speakers are rare. Secondly, those who are good are thrust into positions of leadership. Also, eloquence suggests qualifications. Anyone who is introduced as a speaker for a program is assumed to be an expert, and if he speaks well, he is thought to be a leader.

The best current example of the power of public speaking may be found in President Reagan. Others in Washington have an understanding of Congress, knowledge of foreign policy, or breadth of government experience. Yet he has been the most popular and influential President since Eisenhower, possibly since Roosevelt.

"Speakership is leadership." As an advertisement for his company or corporation, an articulate spokesperson is an asset. A good speaker may be promoted if only to give him or her more authority or credibility as a representative of the company.

Now, you do not need to have Presidential aspirations in order to benefit from this book. All you need is a willingness to get over awe and anxiety many people feel when given an invitation to make a speech. For making a speech shouldn't be an ordeal. It's an opportunity—an opportunity for advancement, promotion, and recognition. Once you read and learn my strategies for communication, the chance to speak which you used to fear will now become fun . . . and possibly very profitable.

Part I

WHAT YOU NEED TO BRING
THEM TO THEIR FEET

Chapter 1

Three Ways to Control Speaking Jitters

Do any of you readers lack a college education? By that I mean you didn't even attend college for a year or even a semester! Or do you suffer from an embarrassing lisp that makes you an object of ridicule or a halting stutter that makes you an object of pity? Or have you ever fainted out of fear while addressing an audience?

Well, if you put all these handicaps together, it spells the background of Winston Churchill. Though his father, Lord Randolph, was a "first" at Oxford—which is equivalent to Phi Beta Kappa at Harvard—Winston Churchill didn't have the grades to be accepted by any university. So despite a basket of honorary degrees accumulated years later from universities all over the world, he never graduated from any university—or even attended one.

In his youth his stutter turned a ten-minute talk into a twenty-minute ordeal. To correct his pronounced lisp he consulted a top oral surgeon in London, Sir Felix Semon.

Sir Felix told him, "No operation would remove your impediment, and my advice to you is never to undertake a trade or occupation where speaking is a necessary part of making a living."

But Churchill did not heed the advice. He entered politics and was elected to Parliament in 1990. In one of his first speeches he collapsed from nervous anxiety in the House of Commons.

Rather than let his deficiency defeat him, Churchill determined to become an impressive speaker. First off, he had to overcome his fear of speaking. He likened the fear of facing a strange audience to the fear of a soldier in facing gunfire. As an officer, he had to display courage before his men, and he reasoned that similarly he could also hide his fear before an audience.

Project Confidence

As a speaker you shouldn't hold onto the lectern as if it is a life raft. Neither should you refuse to look at your audience as if your listeners are a crowd of Gorgon-headed Medusas. Nor should you race through your speech at top speed as if you're running through a gauntlet of pirate swords.

Act confidently by looking out at your audience and by speaking at a deliberate pace. And above all, never apologize for your inability as a public speaker or your insufficiency of preparation or your unfamiliarity with the topic. You would do well to adopt the credo of the British Foreign Service officer: "Never excuse, never explain, never complain."

By apologizing at the outset, you are not taking out an insurance policy for failure; you are only planting the perception of failure with your audience. If you don't tell them, they probably won't find out.

Master Your Material

And secondly, you not only want to *mask* the *mannerisms* that suggest fear, you also want to *master* the *material* which reduces fear.

It is interesting to note that Churchill did not collapse during his maiden speech to the House of Commons, but in his second address. In his first talk, he spoke on his experience as a war correspondent during the Boer War and the lessons he observed from that conflict. The speech was well-received.

In his second speech he attempted a broadside on a whole range of administration policies by the Conservative Government. On this occasion he faltered in the midst of his presentation when he forgot the lines of his memorized text. The lapse caused him to splutter and then swoon to the floor.

If you carefully prepare yourself in your subject, you should know more than any of your listening audience at the time of your presentation. That fact alone should go a long way to reduce your anxiety. Whatever else, you will have enlightened your audience on a subject they know dimly about—whether it is briefing them on a complex law or explaining to them the subtleties of fly casting.

Focus Your Subject

The trick in picking a subject is to pick only a corner of that topic. A daughter of a friend of mine had to write a 100-word paper for a sixth grade project. She decided on the "History of World War II"! I told her she would be better advised to select one battle—or, better yet, one day in the battle, or perhaps even one particular unit in that battle, the infantry or the tank battalion or maybe even the fight for one hill in that battle. (Such advice is well worth remembering by college students too. If you write on something outside the professor's general knowledge, he won't be able to second-guess you, and he will appreciate your recounting something he never knew before.)

My daughter, who was a classics major at Harvard, earned an A by writing on the subtle changes in footwear in the costumes shown in vase design that evolved during the Hellenistic age. By picking an obscure "corner of a subject," she made herself an "expert."

Some of my seminar students tell me that occasionally it is impossible to pick your own subject—the inviting group selects it for you. They ask you to speak on "What's Happening in Washington" or "The Latest in the Bond Market." Well, the answer is you must pare down that broad subject to bite-size proportions. You might want to focus your Washington talk on new laws affecting real estate or agriculture. For the bond speech you might decide to concentrate on the various ratings of city or school bonds. On rare occasions you might even have to disregard completely the speech suggestion of the group and talk on something about which you are an expert.

One time I was invited to speak by a state banker's group. When I arrived at the hotel, I saw a notice posted on the hotel's bulletin board, which announced the place and title of the speech:

Banker's Association—Washington Room
James C. Humes—"Fiscal Econometrics in Washington"

After being introduced I told them of some advice I learned while a student at Williams College. I had enrolled in "Survey of the New Testament" not because I was following some divine impulse to be called for service to God, but rather because the professor, a retired Episcopal minister, always gave the same examination each year: "Trace and Delineate the Travels of the Apostle Paul." That meant that we and the rest of the class, most of whom were jocks, could cut Saturday classes with impunity secure in the knowledge that we could ace the final examination question on the travels of the Apostle Paul.

But were we in for a surprise! The good rector on that dark day before our Christmas break wrote on the blackboard instead this question: "Analyze and Criticize the Sermon on the Mount."

Well, most of the class was stunned, but I saw "Tiny," a football tackle whose head was almost as thick as his shoulders, buckle right down and begin to scribble furiously in his blue book. When we returned from Christmas vacation, it was Tiny who received the highest grade, a B+. I asked him, "Tiny, whatever did you write on that question, 'Analyze and Criticize the Sermon on the Mount'?"

Tiny looked at me with big blue eyes and explained in his plodding drawl: "Well, Humes, I wrote, 'Who am I to criticize the words of the Master? Instead, I would like to write about the "Travels of the Apostle Paul".' "

And so I said to my audience of bankers, "Who am I to criticize the words of the Master? Instead I would like to talk about my experience in Washington, which I have entitled, 'Confessions of a White House Ghost'."

Remember that, when you finish your talk, no one takes into account your unfamiliarity with the subject; people don't say, "He did well considering the topic." They just say, "He did well," or more often, "He didn't do well." So choose a subject in which you have some expertise and then focus in on the subject. A woman who had returned from China asked me for help in shaping a speech before a civic group. She had picked as her title "Impressions of Post-Mao China." Since she was a teacher, I suggested she concentrate on education. I further counseled her, "Why don't you narrow it down still further and talk about 'China and the First Grade.' "

When you focus your subject, you are paring it from broad to narrow. The more narrow and more specific the topic, the more likely it will penetrate the listener's mind and take hold. Remember the more you master your material, the more you will be viewed as an expert.

Fear: The Psychological Edge

Some years ago, a magazine conducted a poll on the greatest fears. Number 3 was "death," Number 2 was "cancer" and Number 1—believe it or not—was "Giving a speech." If you master your material you will be able to control your fear. You will never completely eliminate that fear as you rise to face your audience. Churchill never did—why should you!

Nor do you want to! A little fear is the psychological edge that gets your adrenaline moving. If you are completely re-laxed you won't be "up" for your performance. Fear is the spur to study and preparation. "Butterflies are beautiful," and if you channel your fear into focusing on a subject, you will soar as a speaker with all the brightness of an expert. From the chrysalis of the unknown corporate bureaucrat, you will emerge with the charisma of a leader.

Chapter 2

The Churchill Formula

A young member of Parliament once approach Prime Minister Winston Churchill for some advice on speaking. "Prime Minister, will you look over this draft and tell me how I could put more fire into my speech? Churchill scanned it briefly and snorted "Put fire into the speech? My advice to you is to put the speech into the fire!"

As a young man who aspired to Parliament, Churchill studied both the speeches of his father, Lord Randolph, and the other great orators of the House of Commons such as John Hampden, the Elder Pitt, Burke, and Fox. He jotted his notes down for a never completed article entitled, "The Scaffolding of Rhetoric."

Write for the Ear, Not the Eye

It was Churchill's belief that the secret of writing a good speech was writing for the ear—instead of the eye. When you read this page, your eye fixes on every word, but if you were listening to deliver the same words in a talk, some of the words would either miss delivery to your ear or be misheard.

No transmission tube carries the speaker's words from his mouth to the listener's ear. Many fall off along the way. The conceit of every speaker is that the listener is receiving word by word, sentence by sentence, paragraph by paragraph, as he or she delivers it. That conceit is fatal. Most journalists do not make good speech writers because they have not learned to write for the ear. They fail to appreciate the different capacity for receptivity between the eye and the ear.

One morning while waiting for various members of his Cabinet to assemble for a meeting, Churchill looked over at the minister seated on his right who was quickly scanning a text of his speech he was going to deliver that evening and growled, "Minister, that's a bad speech." "Prime Minister," replied the distraught minister, "how can you tell—surely you can't read upside down!"

"I can tell," rumbled Churchill, "because there are no dashes and dot-dot-dots in the speech, and a speech without dashes and dot-dot-dots is an article, not a speech."

What Churchill meant was that a speech should have the rhythm of conversation. The dashes and dot-dot-dot are punctuation of a radio script, and Churchill, who like Roosevelt mastered the medium of radio, drafted his speeches like radio scripts.

The point is that the ear is about one quarter to one tenth the organ the eye is in retaining impressions. To my seminar classes, I liken a good speech to an article by comparing a tensor light to a regular lamp. A tensor light covers a smaller area but more intensely. In a speech you cannot convey as much material as you would in an article of the same length. Good speeches must be highly focused, direct, and graphic.

Churchill's Five Principles

To craft a speech to meet the lesser organ of the ear, Churchill stressed five principles:

- Strong Beginning
- One Dominant Theme
- Simple Language
- Use of Analogy or Illustration
- Emotional or Dramatic Ending

Strong Beginning

Churchill never began his speech by saying, "It is an honor . . . or "It is a pleasure . . ." He once said, "There are few activities from which I derive intense pleasure and speaking is not one of them." Too many opening amenities are opening inanities. How did Churchill begin in 1940 when leadership was thrust upon him in those dark days for Britain?

> I speak to you for the first time since became Prime Minister, and I would say to the House, as I said to those who have joined this Government, "I have nothing to offer but blood, toil, tears, and sweat."

That is not an "opening amenity."

One Dominant Theme

Churchill compared a speech to a symphony. The three or four movements might play variations on one melodic theme. Of course, a speech might have as many as three or four points, but those points should be embraced by one theme (e.g., "Peace through strength,"

11

"Growth through research," and "Expansion through deregulation.")

In fact, Churchill even went so far as to suggest that you should write the last part of the speech first in order that you know in the beginning where you are heading. Or, better yet, write out in big block letters the theme or central message in one sentence.

When it came to speech writing President Eisenhower was a five-star general. While reading a draft of his speechwriter's efforts, he would tap his pencil impatiently on his desk and say, "What's the Q.E.D.?" (a geometry term meaning *Quod Erat Demonstrandum* —"Which was to be proved"). Eisenhower was saying in effect, "What is the bottom line? What is it you want the audience to do when the speech is over?" If you don't have that clearly in mind, you should never begin writing a speech.

An eloquent speech, as well as a memorable book or fine portrait, should emphasize one theme. The multitude of details in a speech, many chapters in a book, or varied colors in a painting should all blend to project on theme.

Simple Language

Not for Churchill was the stilted language of the bureaucrat or technocrat. Once, a functionary from Whitehall reprimanded Churchill for his breezy style. "I was rather shocked, Prime Minister, that you terminated one sentence with a preposition." Churchill retorted, "That is pedantic nonsense up-with-which-I-shall-not-put."

One morning while waiting for various members of his cabinet to assemble for a meeting, Churchill looked over at the minister seated on his right who was quickly scanning the text of a speech he was to deliver that evening.

Churchill growled, "Minister, that's a bad speech." "Prime Minister," replied the distraught minister, " How can you tell—surely you can't read upside down!" "I can tell," rumbled Churchill, "because there are no dashes and dot-dot-dots in the speech, and a speech without dashes and dot-dot-dots is an article, not a speech,"

The point of these two examples is that stuffy syntax, complicated and self-important words, and any other such painting of one's language will not make a speech any better. Language that is clear, concise, and that communicates directly what you have to say, will make for a good one.

Use of Analogy or Illustration

Churchill knew that abstractions such as "undercapitalization," "depreciation," or "balanced budget," go through one ear and out the other without forming a vivid lasting impression in the mind. That is why Churchill, who was a painter by avocation, always tried to draw at least one picture in a talk that would depict the problem or the central idea.

Churchill loved to draw analogies from the animal world. The British Commonwealth was "the old Lion with her cubs." Mussolini was a "jackal" in attacking France. Hitler and Nazi Germany were compared to a "boa constrictor who would befoul his prey with saliva before engorging it."

The Emotional or Dramatic Ending

Finally, Churchill liked to end his speech dramatically with an appeal to the emotions. Often he would close his dramatic appeal with a bit of verse or a poignant experience. In a 1941 radio address, when he was asking for aid from the United States, he did both.

> The other day I received a letter from President Roosevelt, delivered to me by his opponent in the last Presidential election and in it there was a poem written in his own hand—by Longfellow—which he said "applies to you people as it does to us."

> *"Sail on, O Ship of State!*
> *Sail on, O Union, strong and great!*
> *Humanity with all its fears*
> *And all the hopes of future years,*
> *Hangs breathless on thy fate!"*

And then Churchill said, "What is the answer I shall give to America? Here it is: Give us the tools, and we will finish the job!"

Churchill has given us the tools for selling a message and persuading an audience. *Strong beginning, one theme, simple language, arresting analogy* and *emotional ending.* If you follow these principles, you will craft a fine talk and be a leader as well as a communicator.

Chapter 3

A Menagerie of Mistakes to Avoid

Picture yourself in Noah's Ark. Noah, of course, wanted to preserve all of the species. But imagine, if you will, that the seas become choppy and that Noah tells you to find and get rid of some of the beasts for the safety of the ship as well as the passengers.

Such a task is much like editing your first draft of a speech. In the previous chapter, "The Churchill Formula," you learned the "offensive" side of preparing your remarks. This rereading and reshaping is the "defensive side."

The Anaconda

The first beast to look for is the *anaconda*. The anaconda is the biggest snake on earth. Its size can run to thirty or forty feet. In speech, *anacondas* are serpentine sentences that strangle the listener's ear.

15

Of course, occasionally a speaker wants to befuddle a questioner with tortuous syntax. President Eisenhower was once asked by a reporter in 1960, "Do the NATO commanders in the field have the authority to dispatch nuclear weaponry?" Eisenhower gave an answer that would make the legendary Casey Stengel seem lucid by comparison. It seemed the subject would never find the predicate in a thousand years even with radar.

At the end of the press conference, Eisenhower turned to his press secretary, Jim Hagerty, and said, "I guess those newspaper fellows will never figure out whether those guys have the authority or not." Eisenhower knew that if he made clear the delegation of authority, it would either be interpreted as warmongering or else it would endanger our threat of retaliation.

But generally the purpose in giving a speech is to communicate not to confuse. Any sentences that are over five lines in the typewritten page are too long. Kill the *anacondas* by chopping them up.

The Coiled Anaconda

Another variation of the problem is the *coiled anaconda*— a subordinate clause put in a single space. Don't say:

> James Humes who has written nine books, one of which was his prize-winning biography, *Churchill Speaker of the Century*, has given seminars on speech communication in four states and eleven countries.

Say instead:

> James Humes has written nine books, one of which was his prize-winning biography *Churchill Speaker of the Century*. He has also given . . .

A Chinese nest of boxes may be pleasing to the eye in the living room, but in the auditorium that kind of subordinate clause construction is hard on the ear.

Complicated syntax with subordinate clauses hatching more subordinate clauses or participial phrases reminds one of those convoluted German or Latin sentences. The audience cannot diagram a complicated sentence in its head as they would on a blackboard in an English grammar class. It is frequently best to have your active verbs early on in the sentence.

The Turtle

Another reptile to look out for is the *turtle*. The slow and plodding turtle is distinguished by his ability to retract his head and hide it underneath his shell. The *turtle* describes the passive voice construction. The passive compared to the active voice is not only more cumbersome—it also robs the listener of information about the actor or perpetrator of the action. Take the sentence, "The jobs will be terminated by December 1." The listener wants to know who is responsible for the firings. The passive voice allows the bureaucrat to duck responsibility.

Some corporate executives like the passive because it seems more complex. They're wrong. The active voice provides force to your speech. The passive voice sounds timid.

As you reread your text, look for variations of the verb "to be"—"is" or "was" or even "have been"—you can be pretty sure it signals the passive voice. The rest of the time it means another variation of the *turtle*, which is the "It is . . ." or "There are" construction. Yes, Shakespeare once wrote, "There is a tide in the affairs of men. . . ." This is the rare good use of that construction. Usually it denotes sloppy writing.

So when you see a variation of the verb "to be," be ready to turn around the passive to active or the "It is necessary" to "we must."

After all Churchill didn't say, "It is obligatory that implements be furnished in order that our assignments can be finalized." He said, "Give us the tools, and we will finish the job." And the American Congress responded to his forceful verbs.

Lincoln did not say, "It was four score and seven years ago that a government was established on this continent." He said, "Four score and seven years ago our fathers brought forth upon this continent a new nation. . . ."

The Mastadon

This mammoth and clumsy beast represents stilted adverbs such as "therefore," "however," "moreover," "nevertheless," and "notwithstanding"—adverbs that make a speech sound like a lawyer's brief. Instead of "therefore," use the one syllable word "so." "But" or "yet" can take the place of "however," "still" can substitute for "nevertheless."

Jettison these polysyllabic monstrosities. The result will be a more conversational talk that will glide more smoothly and swiftly.

Would you say in conversation, "I went to a great restaurant. Moreover, it was cheap?" A more colloquial way is to say, "What's more, it was cheap." The same substitution in a speech makes a bulky style brisk.

Other mastodons include "nonetheless," "notwithstanding," and "inasmuch as." That's the language of a high school debater. Eliminate the mastodons.

The Owl

The next creature is the *owl*. An owl mournfully calls "whoo," "whoo." So does the audience when the speech drafter uses vague pronouns.

A speaker on tariffs might say, "We must tell them that this has to be changed if our industries are going to survive and prosper." By "we" does he mean American people or the steel industry? Does "them" refer to Japan or Congress? Does "this" refer to regulations or quotas?

When I read the novels of Tolstoi or Dostoevski, I put in front of me a sheet with names of all the characters just so I can keep them all straight. In a play the audience has the theater program with the list of the cast. But the audience for a speech has no cast of personalities to refer to. That's why the speaker must be very precise about "who," "we," "them," "it," etc. Remember this maxim. In writing prose, repetition — called redundancy — is considered a vice. In speaking, it is a device.

The Dinosaur

Perhaps the ugliest creature to watch out for is the Dinosaur. The Dinosaur was once the biggest, longest creature on earth. Dinosaur words occupy a log of space on the page, but their impact is smaller than their size. Perhaps because of their size, dinosaurs hold much fascination. Similarly, government officials and business executives love to use dinosaur words to attract attention and to impress. "Bureaucratese" or "corporatese" loads up with dinosaurs. Some of these dinosaur words include the use of the noun "impact" as a verb, "to impact on," or the trendy adjective "proactive," which is supposed to describe planning initiatives to prevent difficulties or emergencies, which then have to be "reacted to." Churchill once said that Ramsay MacDonald used words "huge in size but tiny in meaning." Such are "dinosaurs."

Eisenhower once suggested that Churchill read over the general's speech. When Sir Winston finished, he harumphed, "Dwight, it has too many passives and too many zeds." In the latter instance, Churchill was referring to what the Americans call the letter "zee," which is most commonly found in the verb suffix "-ize," employed to turn nouns or adjectives into verbs. (Actually the British use "ise" — e.g., "realise"). "Finalize" and "prioritize" are two popular abominations of the bureaucratic set. Former Secretary of State Alexander Haig might have spawned a new *dinosaur* horror record when he uncorked the word "agendize."

My pet hate of a *dinosaur* is that staple of technocrats, the verb "interface," which to me describes something I'd like to do with Meryl Streep! It is a bureaucratic or corporate version of "talk to" or "discuss with." Only a little less objectionable is the use of "dialogue" as a verb, e.g., "perhaps we should dialogue with labor."

Another variation of the *dinosaur* is the inflated euphemism. "Euphemism" derives from a Greek term meaning "use of words of good omen." In modern usage it means "alternate meaning and usually a softer one." One example of this was a report from a New York hospital in which they announced that in certain operation, "negative outcomes had decreased."

How would the Lord's Prayer sound, "Yea though I walk through the valley of negative outcome . . ."?

In Pentagonese, an officer refers to the dead and wounded left on the battlefield as "inoperative military personnel." The CIA labels assassinations "termination with extreme prejudice." The Congressman designates a tax increase a "revenue enhancement." The alderman calls garbage collectors "sanitary engineers."

Still other variations of the *dinosaur* are bureaucratic acronyms such as OSHA (Occupational Safety and Health Agency) or AID (Agency for International Development). The one sounds like something nautical and the other like something medical.

Speeches filled with alphabet soup do not impress the audience. That holds true for all *dinosaurs* that are corporatese or bureaucratese. So every time you see lots of initials or "zees" in your speech text, you are seeing the footprints of a dinosaur. Keep them off the craft that is your text.

The Lame Duck

Another animal to shoo off the boat is the *lame duck*. The *lame duck* describes a verb that cannot carry its own weight.

John Kennedy once said, "We must maintain vigor." "Maintain" is a bad word here, for it doesn't go with "vigor." "We must fight hard" is a stronger way of promising action. Churchill did not say, "We will maintain a defense in the beaches, we will maintain a defense on the landing grounds . . ."

"Sustain," which is rhyming brother of "maintain," is another *lame duck*. "We will sustain a major offensive." Why not say "mount" or "unleash"? "The enemy has sustained setbacks." Isn't "we have inflicted injury" better?

Other weak verbs are "involve" and "entail."

The mediocre speaker will say, "This is going to entail a lot of research before we . . ."

A leader will say instead, "We are going to read, study, and analyze this proposal before we. . . . "

Lame duck verbs like "engage" are wimp verbs that cannot fly and force the nouns to act in their place.

The Sheep Dog

The noun equivalent of the *lame duck* is the *sheep dog*, a glob of fluff that represents the vague collective noun. No one can see the true shape of a *sheep dog* because all his hair hides it. Does the *sheep dog* underneath that hirsute mass resemble a setter or airedale or what?

In a speech, the phrase "human resources" is a *sheep dog*. It is a vague abstraction which, though it tries to exalt, only denigrates the diverse skills, talents, and abilities of the American worker.

I once heard a chief executive of a national corporation say, "We are vitally interested in each layer of our corporate personnel." Well, if I had been an employee, I would not have been very happy to be described as a "layer!"

He should have said, "We are proud of the whole team—briefcase toting executives in the corporate headquarters, the white-coated researcher in the lab, the traffic controllers at their phones and desks, the salesmen on the road, and of course, most important, the tireless worker on the production line."

The head of a national insurance company gave a speech to a community civic group. He said, "In the last few years we have been providing instruction as well as advice to various learning centers." Such a vague collective abstraction robbed the listeners of any true picture of what the insurance company was doing—who it was helping and how.

The insurance company head should have said, "To the local community colleges, we have been offering the service of our executives to teach accounting and business law. To the hospitals, we are sending instructors to teach techniques such as cost-benefit analysis as well as accounting. And at the evening classes of the city university we have recruited instructors to teach adults who want to polish up their executive skills by taking courses in marketing or finance."

A favorite *sheep dog* of the corporate world is "energy resources." Again the speaker should take the time to tick off coal mines, oil wells, natural gas lines, hydroelectric dams and atomic energy plants. Otherwise, the phrase "energy resources" goes in one ear and out the other and does not plant itself visually into the mind's eye.

Speakers justify the all-encompassing collective abstraction because it saves time. *Sheep dogs* may save time, but they steal from the audience the picture of what is happening. A concrete picture of different activities is sacrificed to one collective abstraction.

Speakers may use a *sheep dog* collective phrase as a verbal shorthand only after they have spelled out the specific activities.

The Bat

Another beast to exterminate is the *bat*. You know the phrase "blind as a bat." Certain *bat* words create difficulties because the audience cannot see the speech text in front of the speaker. A trio of words serve as an example. "We are going to raise a building." To the audience it sounds like the opposite. Or if one speaks of "enervating natural gas deposits," it suggests "energizing" instead of "draining."

23

Or if one denounces a plan for its "temerity," it sounds more like "timidity" than the "rashness" it actually is. "Cite" is usually heard as "sight."

Bat words *can* be used for a specific purpose. George Smathers of Florida won a senate seat from Claude Pepper by utilizing *bat* words. Pepper, then a sixty-year-old bachelor, counted as his family a sister who was an actress in New York and a niece who worked on the Senator's Public Works Committee. To take the rural vote in the panhandle of Florida away from Pepper, Smathers concocted this attack:

> My friends, the Good Book tells us that, "Ye shall know the truth, and the truth shall make you free." Well it's incumbent on me to tell you the truth about Claude Pepper. My friends, he is a sexagenarian. Why, my friends, after years of matriculating at Harvard, he now practices celibacy all by himself.
>
> It's matter of public record that he commits nepotism with his own niece. And his sister is a well-known thespian in wicked Greenwich Village. Yes, my friends, Claude Pepper has heterosexual proclivities and id known for his notorious extroversion.

Some words have a tricky reverse spin to them that makes them hot words. A woman who was an assistant secretary of state talked to a veterans group using the phrase "nasty conundrum," and she didn't understand the reason for the snickers in the audience who thought she was referring to a device for sexual hygiene.

On the other hand, Churchill used a *bat* word to advantage when he described Italy's invasion of France as "dastardly," which means "cowardly" but suggests that one's parents were not wed.

One Rubensesque lady who was an alumna of a seminar of mine reported that, while wearing a tight sweater, she had exhorted her listeners repeatedly, "to keep abreast of economic developments in Washington." The male minds in the audience turned their thoughts from economy to anatomy.

One executive whose speech I monitored spoke of "cutting off an air line." I had to change it to "cutting off the oxygen tube," so that the audience would not think of United or TWA.

A variation of the *bat* is the word easily mispronounced by the speaker. In writing speeches for President Ford we always used the word "atomic" because he would trip over the word "nuclear." (President Ford would always say nook-ke-leer.)

Even more egregious was President Lyndon Johnson, who in reading from a text talked of "horse doves" when the speech writer had written hors d'oeuvres. I heard one bureaucrat come out with "eleemosynary," instead of the word "charitable." In your editing, avoid tongue twisters and remove exotic foreign words.

The Peacock

The next to last animal in this Menagerie of Mistakes is the *peacock*, a bird noted for strutting its plumage proudly. Peacock phrases are those that undermine the speaker's credibility with the audience.

Every time you hear a politician say "I pledge to you" or "If elected, I promise to . . . " your first instinct is to hold onto your wallet.

Some years ago a candidate for Congress went out to address an Indian reservation in New Mexico. As the Indian audience seemed to be responding positively to his speech, the candidate began to wax grandiloquent.

"I am proud to say my family has long been lovers and

admirers of Indian culture." The statement was greeted by some Indians yelling, *"Hoya, hoya!"* The candidate, seeing the effect of his words, grew more expansive. "I have long been sensitive to the special needs of the great 'American' people." Again the cries, *"Hoya, hoya!"* "And I pledge to you," the candidate continued, "when I'm elected to Congress, I will see to it that your priorities are my priorities, and my achievements will be your achievements." A deafening *"Hoya, hoya!"* erupted.

After the talk the chief thanked the candidate for his speech. "It was most enlightening," he said. As they walked across a pasture the chief warned, "Now be careful you do not step in the *hoya*."

"Auditorium" has an interesting etymological history. In ancient days, one type of auditorium was an arena for bull fights. Even today, a lot of "bull" is listened to in auditoriums. *Peacock* phrases like "I pledge to you" or "I'm proud to say" can direct a listener's mind to a state of disbelief. Senator Joseph Biden, in his abortive Presidential campaign, often debased his credibility by saying, "I sincerely believe . . . "

When you hear someone say, "I want to be honest with you," your first reaction is to wonder whether he has been dishonest with you in everything he said up to that point. If that's the case, why should the audience be ready to believe what he says when he predicates it with "I'm going to be honest with you." You can't just say you're being honest (or candid or unselfish). That can only be made clear in the rest of your speech.

I once heard a newly elected CEO give a speech to the company employees. He started by saying that his happiest days were those he had spent on the assembly line. Even if it were true, it comes off as a *peacock* phrase to those who see him driving up every day in a chauffeured Mercedes.

Similarly, I heard another chief executive proclaim to an audience, "What matters most to us in this company is not the profits we make but the product we build."

He would have been better advised to say, "Of course, the profit statement is the bottom line—we have to be accountable to our stockholders. But we take pride in a product that is seen as reliable and safe to consumers all over the world."

Of course, the ultimate peacock phrase is "I'm from the government and I'm here to help you." While that is a joke, variations slip into self-serving speeches by those from corporations as well as the government. "Proud," "honest," "promise" should be alarm bells for possible *peacocks* to be cast out.

The Rabbit

The last beast is the *rabbit*. The *rabbits* multiply. So do statistics. Some people rely on statistics to make their points for them. But the mind rebels at number after number, percentage after percentage. Every time one of those complex numerals appears in your text, you should ask yourself is it really necessary? Will it confirm what you are saying or only confuse the audience? Or are you using it in *order* to confuse the audience? At the end of the book I will give you some tips for using statistics. In the meantime remember the *rabbit* is a beast to be dumped overboard.

Chapter 4

Organizing Your Speech

Sir Winston Churchill, while dining at Claridge's, once asked for his favorite dessert, Sherry Trifle. After tasting the first spoonful, he signaled for the waiter. "Pray, take this pudding away—it has no theme."

Well, Churchill liked his puddings as well as his presentations to hold together, to be consistent—to have one theme.

That laudable goal is not as easily achieved as it sounds. The temptation in any speech is to divert and digress. Points which you think have to be mentioned end up deflecting the audience's attention from the central problem. Sometimes as you start to write your text, you think you won't have enough material to fill your time, and then you end up by writing too long a speech.

Many Congressmen during adjournment return to their constituencies and speak to a local Rotary or Kiwanis Club.

Their talks recount legislative accomplishments and report on the status of certain bills, but the listener is lost in a sea of numbers—H.R. 1042, S. 256—and misses any central message such as recovery, reform, or government waste.

CEO's in their instructions to a speech writer list too many issues to be covered—company history, economic prospects, new products in the future, as well as the outlook in Washington.

At a Dale Carnegie School you may hear a simplistic formula for keeping on one track: Tell them what you are going to say—say it—and then tell them what you have said. Well, that formula at least insures you of getting your message directly across.

Pitcher Johnny Sain of the Boston Braves in his rookie year was facing the great Rogers Hornsby of the St. Louis Cardinals at the plate. Sain, trying to be cute, aimed for the corner of the plate. Bill Klem, the umpire, called it a ball. Sain didn't like the call, but he tried nibbling at the corners again. Again Klem said, "Ball." Sain protested. Klem said, "Young man, when you throw a strike, Mr. Hornsby will let you know it."

Klem knew that the future Hall of Famer Hornsby would squarely hit any ball that was in the strike zone. And in a speech you want to hit your message squarely. To help you do that, I'm offering you an acronym SQUARE.

Statement
Quotation
Umbrella
Anecdote
Repetition
Ending

Statement

First, do as Churchill suggested and write out a statement that sums up the message of your talk. Do that before you outline your points and begin writing your text. It will help you focus on that central theme. You don't have to begin your speech with that sentence. In fact it is best if you don't. Plenty of opportunities will arise for you to insert that key sentence as you organize your talk.

Such a key sentence might be "A strong defense prevents war" or "If good schools mean jobs, good teachers mean good education."

Quotation

Second, find a quotation that fortifies and backs up that sentence or statement:

> Senator Henry Jackson said, "The Soviet Union is like a hotel burglar who checks every room to see if it is locked."

> Henry Adams in his *Education of Henry Adams* said, "The influence of a teacher never stops—it affects eternity."

Umbrella

Third, even if you have several points to make about defense (budget, arms negotiation with the Soviets, Strategic Defense Initiative) or education (federal aid, lack of school discipline, the drug problem, teacher certification) make sure you tailor them to fit under the *umbrella* of your key statement. Shape or trim discussion of those issues so that they are neatly covered by the central statement or theme. If you don't, you will find that overexpansion on a point will not only muddy and dampen that topic but soak through and dampen the effect of the key theme. And if you find you can't shorten or shape those points, you may have to get yourself a bigger umbrella.

Anecdote

Fourth, find an *anecdote* or an *analogy* that depicts or delivers your main theme or message. Here are two examples:

> During the Constitutional Convention in 1787 when it was proposed that the National Army be limited to 3,000 men, George Washington whispered from his presiding chair, "Then we should have another article providing that no foreign nation with an army exceeding 3,000 men be allowed to invade."

> In 1975, President Ford hosted a ceremony honoring outstanding teachers. To a teacher from North Carolina, he said, "I understand that you the teach fifth grade."
>
> "No, Mr. President, I don't teach the fifth grade—I teach children!"

Repeat

Fifth, you must not be afraid to repeat your theme. I remember the advice Fred Fox, a one-time Congregational preacher and Eisenhower speech writer, told me. "Repetition may be a vice in prose but in speeches it is a device." After the discussion of each point, you might want to repeat the main theme and tie that particular point to the central message. The apt quotation or interesting anecdote are two ways to repeat the theme. Similarly the clever analogy or documented case example are other ways to emphasize the central theme. So is a clear statement that consolidates all the various points under one *umbrella.*

Ending

Finally, the *ending* offers one last chance to stress the speaker's message. If you fail to sound the dominant theme at the close, you run the risk that your audience will not grasp your message. That final dramatic close—whether it includes a hopeful description offered by the resolution of the problem or a dramatic appeal for action—must be linked to the central message:

> Sometimes I have ended a speech this way. "Good will or good intentions are not a substitute for action. We need a change in the by-laws now. We can't wait until the convention three years from now. When George Washington was positioned by the Hudson River in 1779, he called in a general known as "Mad Anthony" Wayne.
> Said Wayne: "I'll storm Hell, General Washington, if you will only plan the assault." And Washington replied, "Perhaps my dear General Wayne, we had better try Stony Point first."

Similarly the speaker must frame his theme in a statement, reinforce it by quotation, analogy, or example, and finally restate it in his closing appeal to the audience.

Chapter 5

Making Use of Parables and Pictures

On Sunday television, words such as "redemption," "salvation," and "grace" spill from evangelists who preach on gospel programs. Yet Jesus of Nazareth seldom dealt in theological abstractions. Though they filled the letters of the Apostle Paul, they rarely appeared in Jesus' sermons.

To illustrate "salvation" or "redemption" Jesus told the story of the prodigal son who wasted his inheritance on wine, women, and song and then, when stripped of means and station, asked his father to give him shelter. The father forgave him and restored him to his position in the family.

Jesus' use of parables to reveal his message owed much to his Talmudic education, in which a story or anecdote was a frequent rabbinical device. The Greek-trained Paul did not use the "parable." In a short written text a story might be too expansive, but in the oral talk the outline of a story will be remembered long after the exact words are forgotten.

In Jesus' audiences few, if any, had the literate capacity to write down his sermons. Yet fifty years after his death witnesses could recount the gist of Jesus' messages to those assembling what is now the New Testament. People love a good story, and those aged survivors of his followers could remember the Parable of the Talents, the Parable of the Mustard Seed, the Good Samaritan, and many others.

Aristotle once wrote that the most difficult problem in writing rhetoric is finding the analogy or metaphor to illustrate a point or problem. Perhaps it was for a Greek who waited for the Muse to touch his brow. But it is not if you will but tap your own memory.

One of the greatest American speeches ever delivered was "Acres of Diamonds." The address, delivered 6,000 times all over the United State,s won for it originator, Russell Conwell, fame and fortune, and the proceeds built the university in Philadelphia now known as Temple. Conwell told his listeners that the stuff of success was not to be found in faraway mines or distant climes but in their own backyard, in their own realm of experience.

Similarly, to develop an analogy, you don't have to ransack the library for anecdote books. You can extract anecdotes from your own life.

Don't wait for the Muse of Inspiration to strike. Jot down a brief tag line of the stories or incidents you have recounted to your family and friends about college, the war, your job, or your childhood.

Write down on a sheet of paper under the headings of "job," "family," "childhood," "school," "dating," "travels," "recreation," "vacation," "restaurants," and think of every story those headings trigger in your memory. What did you learn from your first date? What advice did your grandfather give you? What did your football coach tell you when you missed a tackle?

All those stories have a point. It could be planning, patience, tolerance, and initiative, or perhaps the importance of timing, the problem of communication, the necessity of education or the wisdom of experience.

Outline these stories briefly with just a phrase or two to recall the incident and then label it under a heading. Just the very process of writing them down and cataloging them will expand your storehouse of anecdote and analogy.

But if in a speech you still find yourself researching for the right story to illustrate your point, just think of the word PICTURES. This acronym stands for

Parents
Interests
Chores
Television
University
Recreation
Environment
Shopping

Parents

For an example, I remember as a child my brother and I would slice and hand-squeeze the oranges for morning juice. One morning my brother and I were throwing around the oranges like baseballs, and a misfired toss smashed a Bohemian sherry decanter.

Since my throw caused the breakage, I had to present the bad news to my mother. I said, "Mom, you know the decanter that you said had been passed down generation to generation in our family? Well, our generation just dropped the ball!" I use this story to bring home the point of missing an opportunity or failing a responsibility.

Interests

For *interests* I often turn to my hobby of collecting autographs—or rather letters or documents with autographs—of historic or literary greats. Factors in evaluating autographs include the date or the rarity of the notable's signature. But the worth of an autograph is often not so much determined by the fame and stature of the notable as by the content of the letter or paper. Can Grover Cleveland's autograph be more valuable than George Washington's? Yes, if the Washington autograph is merely his signature on a commission while the letter by Grover Cleveland is a letter to his law partner. In other words, the message may be more important than the bearer of the message.

I have used this illustration in speeches to counteract the authority of famous names, who express opinions on subjects about which they may have little or no experience.

Chores

For *chores* I have used the procedure for mowing a lawn. The mower begins on the outside of the perimeter and works toward the heart. I used this example in a State Department speech, saying that in the area of confrontation between the United States and the Soviet Union, we would trim and reduce the potential scope for conflict by starting to negotiate peripheral disputes, such as fishing rights or trade issues. These agreements would narrow the area of contention and strengthen faith in the negotiating process.

Television

Television, as well as movies, is a rich source of images. On occasion I have used Clark Gable's line to Vivien Leigh in *Gone with the Wind*, "Frankly, my dear, I don't give a damn." When you depict a great actor or actress in a familiar scene, you immediately send a picture to the listener's mind, which reinforces your point. One of my favorites is recalling the late Peter Finch in the movie *Network*, when he rolled up his window in his skyscraper suite and screamed, "I'm mad as hell." But whether it is Clark Gable to show apathy or Peter Finch to reflect anger, scenes from movies or television can dramatize your points.

University

University or school days trigger good speech examples. I remember going back to my twenty-fifth college reunion. I walked into the class of my old economics professor and discovered he was asking the same questions he asked our generation of students a quarter of a century ago.

When I confronted the professor after the class, he admitted it, saying, "Yes, Humes, same questions, but I'm expecting different answers." I have employed that encounter to emphasize that in many cases old solutions do not work and that we need new approaches to problems of poverty or crime.

Recreation

Recreation or sports bring back scores of vivid memories. Yogi Berra provides two unintentional profundities that lend themselves to speech points. Once he said of a popular restaurant, "No one goes there anymore because it is too crowded." Another Berra adage etched in my mind was, "You observe a lot of things just by watching." Golfers and sailors can draw on all kinds of examples—such as sizing up the lie of your ball to assess what kind of shot you can try—alternative approaches or solutions. Or how by tacking your boat against the wind you can reach your destination—to show how a disadvantage or difficulty can be turned into an opportunity.

When I was an eleven year old, I had the opportunity of meeting Branch Rickey. He told me that he scanned the minor league box scores in the *Sporting News* for two items having to do with the number "3"—third base and triples. Said Rickey, "If a player is a good third baseman, it means he has a very strong arm. The third baseman has to throw across the diamond to first base. He could be switched to catcher, shortstop, outfield, or even pitcher, all positions that require sturdier arms than, say, the first or second baseman. Then if he hits a lot of triples, it means he has speed as well as power." From this story I drew the conclusion that the most meaningless or trivial statistic can herald a movement or a trend.

Environment

Another fertile source for pictures is the *environment* or weather. All of you have experienced the lull before a storm. One of your friends might have related to you his witnessing of a hurricane. Since he was in the eye of the hurricane, he was safe. A lesson of turning into a skid while driving a car may be used to explain your purchase of stocks, or buying short in the market.

The deep blizzard in the winter of 1958 closed down the State Department for five days, including a weekend. Queries on how to handle certain situations in foreign capitals went unanswered. In the delay no action was taken. The result was that, in all seven pressing cases—including an impending coup d'état, a possible violent demonstration, and the prospective termination of a military base contract—no action worked out to be the *right* action. In other words, sometimes we would be better off to let things work out by themselves instead of playing a heavy hand.

Shopping

The final letter of the acronym is *shopping*. As consumers we make hundreds of decisions each year in purchasing a home or a car or in choosing the right insurance package. Each of the decisions might involve strategies for evaluation or bargaining. Here's how *shopping* can be used to point up your message

> I recall last summer seeing a man browsing through the supermarket picking up condiments at one counter, cheese spreads at another, and gourmet ice cream at the dairy section as he piled his basket full. When he came to the checkout counter, he started to add up his purchases mentally. The amount staggered him, and he sheepishly went back, depositing some of his high ticket luxury items to their respective shelves. This obvious summer bachelor had not made out a list of the priority items the way his wife would. We all need

a plan, whether it is in shopping for groceries or determining a federal budget.

Sir Joshua Reynolds, the great British portrait artist and master of reproducing subtle tones of flesh and clothes, was once asked, "What do you mix your colors with?" His reply was quick: "With brains."

Well, you, as a speaker, must mix your brains with colors. You must paint pictures for your audience—pictures that demonstrate your ideas and conclusions.

Chapter 6

How to Add Zingers and Ringers

President Ronald Reagan may be the Great Communicator of his time, but one wonders how many of his statements will grace the pages of *Bartlett's Quotations*. In contrast, Franklin Roosevelt and John Kennedy boast at least a page apiece.

Think to yourself. Can you recall any memorable words by Reagan? "Make my day" originated in a Clint Eastwood movie, and his 1980 election-debate retort to Jimmy Carter, "There you go again," is more slang than substance.

Roosevelt in his inaugural address said, "The only thing we have to fear is fear itself." Almost everybody can quote the line from John Kennedy's inaugural: "Ask not what your country can do for you; rather ask what you can do for your country."

The inaugural of Ronald Reagan in 1981 provided all the right staging to put a quotable line in neon lights: handsome, charismatic President, ushering in a new era. One of his lines also had the ring of a catchy statement: "If we love our country, why should we not also love our countrymen?"

Yet it failed to capture national attention. Why? Because Reagan did not set it up. If Reagan has any failing as a speaker, it is his reluctance to use a lead-in statement to set up the quotable or memorable.

In 1933, Franklin Roosevelt said, "Let me again assert my firm belief [pause] that the only thing we have to fear is fear itself." Note the "Let me again assert . . ." It is redundant, of course, when he says he is giving his "firm belief." To do otherwise is an insult to his audience. Surely he is not giving them his tentative beliefs!

John Kennedy in his inaugural address said, "And so, my fellow Americans, ask not. . . ." Who did Kennedy think he was talking to—Frenchmen or Germans? Churchill said, *"I would say to the House* as I told those who joined the government [pause] that the only thing I have to offer you is blood, toil, tears, and sweat."

Any prefatory line such as "Ladies and Gentlemen," "I say to you," "Let me say again," "I submit to you" are lead-in lines used to call attention to the key sentence following them. Such a filler line is the means by which a speaker can call attention to a quotable statement or slogan. A speaker cannot underline or put in block letters a phrase or statement in his or her text. The prefatory statement followed by a pause is the orator's way of using Magic Marker to underline a sentence. (A prefatory line is not to be confused with "the opening amenity" such as "It is a pleasure . . ." or "It is an honor. . . .")

Reagan does not use this technique. Perhaps he finds it too stagy. He prefers to set up lines by his own masterful sense of timing and inflection. But if Reagan editorially deletes attempts by his speech writers to call attention to their favorite crafted lines, that is no reason why you should. If you craft a catchy line, a witty slogan, or a punchy statement, frame it by setting it up first with a prefatory statement and then that pregnant pause.

A quotable line rises to the top the way cream does in a milk bottle. CREAM is an acronym to explain what makes a sentence eminently quotable.

Contrast
Rhyme
Echo
Alliteration
Metaphor

Contrast

Churchill said in 1940, "If we open a quarrel between the past and present, we shall find we have lost the future." His most famous use of "contrast" was his attack on the Baldwin government in 1936. "Decided only to be undecided, resolved to be irresolute, adamant for drift, solid for fluidity, all powerful to be impotent."

"The law in its majestic equality," said Anatole France, "forbids all men to sleep under bridges, to beg in the streets, and to steal bread—the rich as well as the poor." "Future and Past," "Rich and Poor," "Mountains and Valleys," "White and Black," "Old and Young" all provide the stuff of quotability. The Beatitudes in Jesus' Sermon on the Mount reflect the use of contrast: "Blessed are the poor in spirit for theirs is the kingdom of heaven." So does the Kahlil Gibran, a favorite of the teenage set. "Let there be spaces in your Togetherness," "I have learned silence from the talkative, toleration from the intolerant, and kindness from the unkind." Martin Luther King, Jr., said in 1963, "Injustice anywhere is a threat to justice every-where."

In 1940, Churchill used contrast when he said, "Never in the field of human conflict was so much owed by so many to so few." Adlai Stevenson said, "The time to stop revolution is at the beginning not the end." John Kennedy said, "To state facts frankly is not to despair of the future or indict the past." "Government is not the answer but the problem" is another quotable use for contrast.

Rhyme

Rhyme is a frequent rhetorical ploy used and sometimes abused by Jesse Jackson: "From the courthouse to the statehouse, from the *statehouse* to the *White House* . . . "

Churchill used rhyme in his Iron Curtain statement when he said, "From Stettin in the *Baltic* to Treiste in the *Adriatic*." He rhymed when he described Field Marshall Montgomery as: in defeat, *indomitable*, in advance, *invincible*, and in victory, *insufferable*.

Roosevelt used rhyme when he vetoed a tax bill by saying, "It is not a tax bill but a tax relief bill, providing relief not to the *needy* but the *greedy*."

Adlai Stevenson in his acceptance speech in 1952 at the Democratic Convention said, "Let's talk sense to the American people. Let's tell them the truth, that there are no g*ains* without *pains*."

Nixon in 1969 said, "Let us move from the age of *confrontation* to the age of *negotiation*." Kennedy in 1961 said, "We prefer World law in the age of self-*determination*. We reject world war in the age of mass *extermination*.

Echo

Echo is the name I give to a line that repeats or "echoes" a word or phrase.

In the Gettysburg Address, Lincoln closed with " . . . that government *of the people, by the people,* and *for the people* shall not perish from the earth."

Adlai Stevenson used the echo technique when he said, "Too many confuse being *free* with being *free* and easy." Churchill employed the same technique when he wrote, "A fanatic is one who can't *change* his mind and won't *change* the subject." Rhetoricians might term Churchill's repetition of the same verb as zeugma.

Roosevelt's famous inaugural line uses echo. In "The only thing we have to fe*ar* is *fear* itself," the word "fear" is echoed.

In John Kennedy's inaugural, the whole phrase was echoed, *Ask not what your country can do for you; rather ask what you can do for your country.* This reversal of the echo phrase was a frequent technique of his speech writer, Ted Sorenson.

Kennedy used it again in the same address when he said, "Let us *never negotiate out of fear* but let us *never fear to negotiate.*"

Alliteration

Alliteration has always been used if not overused by orators for polishing a line. President Lyndon Johnson alliterated in his address accepting the Presidential nomination in 1964. "This nation, this generation, in this hour has man's first chance to build a great society, a place where the meaning of man's life matches the marvels of man's labor."

Martin Luther King said, "I have a dream . . . that my four little children will one day live in a nation where they will not be judged by the color of their skin but by the content of their character."

Metaphor

Metaphor or simile is the final quotable technique. Here the effect depends not on the sounds of the words but rather on the picture it evokes in the minds. Churchill used the metaphor to denounce appeasers after Munich. "An appeaser is one who feeds the crocodile hoping it will eat him last."

Roosevelt in 1941 defending Lend Lease said, "When you see a rattlesnake poised to strike, you do not wait until he has struck before you crush him."

Harry Truman used this simile to describe the White House. "Being a President is like riding on a tiger. A man has to keep on riding or be swallowed."

The playwright Henrik Ibsen uses this simile, "A community is like a ship—everyone ought to be prepared to take the helm."

CREAM rises to the top, and any one of these devices— *contrast, rhyme, echo, alliteration, metaphor*— could make a sentence rise from the forgettable to the quotable. So try to coin at least one zinger in a speech. To do so, write out the theme of a speech, or the central problem or solution.

Then play with these sentences to see if you can make them more quotable. Let your mind wander mentally through the zoo and see if you can't come up with a good metaphor.

Buy your own *Bartlett's Quotations*. Churchill recommended buying it. He was given a copy of the book by his mother, as I was when I was eighteen, and he pored over the quotations in order to have "them gathered upon my memory." Look up key words in the index and see if you cannot improve on a line previously said. I marked Harry Emerson Fosdick's line, "Democracy is based upon the conviction that there are extraordinary possibilities in ordinary people." I have written for various candidates, "The greatness of democracy is not measured by one or two extraordinary men but rather by ordinary men doing things extraordinarily well."

At the British victory in Egypt in 1942, Churchill adapted Tallyrand's, "This is the beginning of the end" (said about Napoleon's defeat at Waterloo) to "This is not the end. It is not even the beginning of the end. But it is, perhaps, the end of the beginning."

You should not "Bidenize" a familiar quotation. Senator Joseph Biden was knocked out of the 1988 Presidential race for using quotations of the notable as his own. There is a fine but distinct line between reshaping and improving quotations of others and stealing them word for word. The line is the difference between research and plagiarism.

Get yourself a *Roget's Thesaurus* or a good synonym book. Search for synonyms for the key nouns in that key sentence that sums up the central problem or outlines the solution. Look for possibilities in alliteration.

Buy a rhyming dictionary. Look for rhymes particularly for the one syllable word and see if you cannot fit two words that rhyme into a sentence. Coining a catchy line is like composing lyrics. Try it—you'll like it. It's fun.

Once I was writing an address for the CEO of a national oil company. The theme of the speech that I took from discussions with the corporation president was this: America should not push the panic button about the energy crisis. This country has more fossil reserves—oil, natural gas, and coal — than any country in the world. What the government should be doing is offering economic incentives to extract those resources.

I looked at "panic." Could I work with that word? "Panic" is a hard word to rhyme. But what about a synonym—"fear," "scare"? "Scare" seemed to present possibilities. Rhymes offer themselves: "bear," "bare," "care," "dare," "fair," "hair," "lair," "where," "stare," "flair," "blare," "glare," etc.

So I worked out this line: "The time has come for the government to stop scaring American people and start daring them."

Of course, one does not begin a paragraph with this line. You do not lead with your quotable line and then trail off. You build up to it:

> Why is the Carter Administration in effect pushing a panic button? We have in America more reserves of natural fossil fuel—coal, oil, and natural gas—than any country in the world. What we don't have is the kind of tax and economic policies that encourage investment to explore, extract, and develop those resources. Ladies and gentlemen, I say to you [pause] the time has come for the government to stop scaring the American people and start daring them.

Note how the prefatory statement and pause are used to set up and spotlight the quotable line. So try coining your own zinger line for your talk.

Chapter 7

Finding Words That Will Dazzle Your Audience

The most colorful words in the English language are not derived from French or Latin. They're from old Anglo-Saxon words. But you don't need to curse in order to speak directly and powerfully.

Take the verbs "get," "make," "hold," "give," and "turn." Latinate cousins of these are "obtain," "produce," "retain," "donate," and "rotate." Some of the other basic verbs are "sit," "stand," "put," and "take." Which of these two sentences sounds like you really mean business? "Let's resist the Soviets," or "Let's stand up to the Soviets." Or compare "We are going to abstain from voting" to "We are going to sit it out."

Verbs that project action strike listeners' ears hard. They are tools of workers and not those who preside at a desk and never get their fingernails dirty. These are verbs that roll up their sleeves and plow right into the task at hand.

49

The Dazzling Dozen

Here are a baker's dozen of these dazzling verbs. Try each of these verbs with various prepositions. See how each combination of verb and preposition spins off an entirely new meaning.

VERB	PREPOSITION
bring	about
do	across
get	against
give	around
go	below
hold	beneath
make	down
put	for
sit	in
stand	on
take	onto
turn	out
work	over
	through
	to
	under
	up
	up to
	up with
	with
	without

With this list you can make up you own zinger or quotable line. Just take one of the verbs and play with various prepositions. This technique often results in a zinger.

Vice President George Bush said, "If we don't *stand up*

to the Marxist tyranny in South America, we will no longer *stand out* as the leader of the free world."

Richard Nixon once said, "For a nation to *hold up* its standard of living, it must *hold down* the rate of inflation."

Senator Ernest Hollings of South Carolina said, "Everyone wants to *bring down* the deficit but no one wants to *bring up* the idea of taxes."

Barbara Bush, the wife of the Vice President, said, "If we are again to *take over* the lead in productivity, we must first *take out* the problem of illiteracy."

Some other uses of the Dazzling Dozen: "Either we *get along* with organized labor or *get out* of the construction business." "We don't have to m*ake up* with Castro to *make our policies respected* in Latin America."

These quickly minted slogans may seem a bit raw out of context, but you must remember that a zinger must always come at the end of a paragraph, having been set up by a lead-in passage, and followed by a prefatory statement such as "I say to you, . . . "

Dazzling dozens are a favorite with songwriters, who often rhyme such words as "make" with "take," "give" with "live," or "go" with "show."

The Rhyming Nine

If the Dazzling Dozen do not rigger a zinger, you might tickle your mind with the Rhyming Nine.

1. *-AIR/-ARE/-ERE:* IMPAIR, REPAIR, BARE, BLARE, CARE, DARE, FARE, FLARE, PARE, RARE, SCARE, SHARE, STARE, THERE, WHERE

   I heard a speaker say at a United Fund Group meeting, "When people *care*, they want to *share*."

2. *-AIN/-ANE/-EIGN:* BRAIN, DRAIN, GAIN, MAIN, PAIN, PLAIN, RAIN, REMAIN, RETAIN, BANE, CANE, WANE, DEIGN

Adlai Stevenson said in his acceptance speech in 1952, "Let's talk sense to the American people. Let's tell them the truth, that there are no *gains* without *pains*."

3. *-EIGHT/-IGHT/-ITE:* HEIGHT, BRIGHT, DE-LIGHT, FIGHT, FLIGHT, INSIGHT, LIGHT, MIGHT, NIGHT, RIGHT, SIGHT, TIGHT, BITE, KITE, QUITE

Churchill's father, Lord Randolph, beat Glad-stone's Liberal Party on the Irish question by coining the slogan: "Ulster with *fight*, and Ulster will be *right*."

4. *-AY/-EIGH:* BAY, DAY, DELAY, FLAY, FRAY, GRAY, MAY, NAY, PAY, PLAY, PRAY, RAY, RE-PAY, SAY, STAY, SWAY, WAY, WEIGH

Reverend Billy Graham preaches, "Those families who *pray* together, *stay* together."

5. *-O/-OE/-OW:* GO, FOE, HOE, BOW, BLOW, CROW, FLOW, GLOW, GROW, KNOW, LOW, MOW, ROW, SHOW, STOW

Benjamin Franklin said, "Leaders who little *know*, little *grow*."

6. *-AKE/-EAK:* BRAKE, FLAKE, FORSAKE, LAKE, MAKE, QUAKE, SAKE, SHAKE, SNAKE, STAKE, TAKE, BREAK

Governor Thomas Kean of New Jersey said, "The greatness of a nation is achieved not by the *takers* in society but by the *makers*."

7. *-EI/-IGH/-UY/-Y:* DIE, LIE, TIE, HIGH, NIGH, SIGH, THIGH, BUY, DEFY, DENY, FRY, FLY, IMPLY, MY, PLY, SLY, TRY, WRY

Josiah Bunting , President of Hampton-Sydney College in Virginia said, "You can't b*uy* your dreams, you *try* them out."

8. *-EARN/-ERN/-URN:* EARN, LEARN, YEARN, STERN, BURN, CHURN, SPURN

The conservative columnist Richard T. Viguerie said, "If you y*earn* for freedom, *learn* to fight for it."

9. *-AIM/-AME:* ACCLAIM, CLAIM, MAIM, PROCLAIM, BLAME, CAME, DEFAME, FAME, FRAME, GAME, LAME, NAME, SHAME, TAME

Senator Kenneth Keating said of the Bay of Pigs fiasco in 1961, "There is no avoiding s*hame* by assigning *blame.*

Rhyme is the favorite of songwriters as well as copy writers. The suffix "tion" is found in thousands of words. The best way to use it is to combine it with alliteration, as in the following "tion"-ending groups of words.

A–TION: ABDICATION, ACCLAMATION, ACCUSATION, ADMINISTRATION, ADMIRATION, AFFIRMATION

Ambassador to the Organization of American States, Dr, Richard T. McCormack, said, "Our policy in Latin America should be *affirmation*, not an *abdication* of the Monroe Doctrine."

C–TION: CALCULATION, COMBINATION, COMMU-
NICATION, CONCENTRATION, CONDEMNATION,
CONSECRATION, CONSOLIDATION, CONSULTA-
TION, CONSUMMATION, COOPERATION, COORDI-
NATION, CORONATION, CORPORATION, CULMINA-
TION

I wrote this line for a congressman who in a press
conference wanted to complain that the White House
had not briefed certain members of Congress. "*Communication* after the fact is no substitute for *consul-
tation* before it."

D–TION: DEDICATION, DELEGATION, DESTINA-
TION, DETERIORATION, DISCRIMINATION, DISIN-
TEGRATION, DISSIPATION

Senator Earnest Hollings of South Carolina said of
Irangate, "There is no *dedication* to duty when there
is *delegation* of that duty."

E–TION: ELEVATION, ELIMINATION, EMULATION,
ESTIMATION, EXALTATION, EXHILARATION, EX-
PECTATION, EXPIRATION, EXPLOITATION

Former Governor John Connally, a Presidential candidate in 1980, said, "The Marxists turn the dreams
of *expectation* into the despair of *exploitation*."

I–TION: IDENTIFICATION, IMITATION, INFLATION,
INFORMATION, INSTALLATION, INVESTIGATION,
IRRITATION, ISOLATION

L–TION: LIBERATION, LIMITATION, LOCATION

The conservative activist Howard Phillips said, "In
the *limitation* of government spells the *liberation* of
man."

M–TION: MEDIATION, MEDITATION, MITIGATION, MUTILATION
I wrote this line for a president of a major auto manufacturer. "*Mediation* begins with the *mitigation* of the rhetoric."

O–TION: OBLIGATION, OBSERVATION, OCCUPATION, ORGANIZATION
Former Governor Raymond Shafer said to the Bar Association in Philadelphia, "What makes a job an *occupation* is the *obligation* to serve the community."

P–TION: PARTICIPATION, PERSPIRATION, POPULATION, PRESENTATION, PROCLAMATION, PROVOCATION, PUBLICATION
Thomas Edison wrote, "Genius is ninety percent *perspiration* and ten percent *inspiration.*"

R–TION: RECREATION, REGULATION, REPUDIATION, REPUTATION, RESERVATION, REVELATION, REVOCATION, ROTATION, RUINATION
For an executive in the American Petroleum Institute I penned the line: Too often the *regulation* of business is followed by the *ruination* of business.

S–TION: SALVATION, STAGNATION, STATION, STIMULATION
Congressman Jack Kemp has preached, "To tax or to cut taxes—that is the choice between *stagnation* or *stimulation* of our economy."

V–TION: VEGETATION, VENERATION, VEXATION, VINDICATION, VIOLATION, VISITATION, VOCATION

Thacher Longstreth, Philadelphia city councilman and former head of the city's Chamber of Commerce, wrote, "The *veneration* of our founding fathers begins with a *visitation* to Independence Hall in Philadelphia."

If you have finished typing out a speech, and no quotable line has emerged from your typewriter, take a break and play around with the Dazzling Dozen or Rhyming Nine. I guarantee that one zinger will present itself for your speech. Then remember to set up your zinger or quotable line with a prefatory phrase such as "I say to you, . . . ," "Let us bear in mind . . . ," or "Let me again assert my firm belief . . . ," followed by a pregnant pause.

Chapter 8

The Art of Quoting

In Pennsylvania a Methodist preacher in the 1930s was about to lose his job. The dwindling few of his congregation who still came to the church fell asleep during his sermons. The church elders came to the pastor and told him of their sad decision. The minister remonstrated and begged for one more chance.

"I can give a great sermon. Just listen to me next Sunday."

The next Sunday the clergyman, true to his word, delivered a captivating, eloquent sermon. The elders met and continued his contract. The head of the elders, as he imparted the good news to the relieved pastor, said:

"You know you certainly delivered a whale of a sermon—there's only one thing that puzzles me. Why did you put up to fingers of your right hand when you started and then two fingers of your left hand when you finished?"

"Oh," said the clergyman somewhat sheepishly, "those were the quotation marks!"

Well, speakers have traditionally borrowed from the writing of politicians, preachers, and poets to back up a claim, stress a point, or refute an argument. John Kennedy, armed with notebooks of quotations collected by his chief aide Ted Sorenson, marched his way through the 1960 primaries and to the Presidency conscripting the services of poets such as T. S. Eliot and Robert Frost, prophets such as Isaiah and Joel, politicians such as Demosthenes and Woodrow Wilson, and historians such as Thucydides and Gibbon. Had Kennedy read the original sources? It didn't matter. The impression conveyed to the public was a new kind of politician whose directions came from books not bosses. This reputation as scholar was enhanced by his biography, *Profiles in Courage*, the chief writing for which was done by Sorenson while Kennedy lay flat on his back in the hospital. Kennedy's father had told his son, "If you write a book, people will respect you and take your judgements seriously."

The ambassador's advice to his son could also apply to quotations. Kennedy was the first President to make *Barlett's* a campaign weapon. If Churchill "mobilized the English language and sent it into battle," Kennedy mobilized the quotations of the great and arrayed them as artillery.

The right quotation is like a distinguished general—slender and erect with the stars of his rank flashing. People don't have an interest in what some obscure professor said about economics or ecology, and they don't have the patience to hear paragraphs by Proust or Plato. They want celebrity combined with brevity.

The frequent speaker must assemble his own file of quotations. Actually it was my own black notebook of quotations (and anecdotes as well) that led me to be chosen as a White House speech writer. In fact, Richard

Nixon once introduced me as "the Quotesmaster General."

If you want some reading assignments to find some good quotations as well as anecdotes, I would suggest the King James version of the Bible—particularly Ecclesiastes, Isaiah, and the other prophets, Psalms and the Proverbs, and perhaps the Matthew and Luke gospels in the New Testament. Shakespeare should be read, particularly the tragedies (Lincoln as well as Churchill knew large portions of them by heart), and in addition Emerson's essays (for speaking style as well as quotations), Carl Sandburg's biography of Lincoln, Martin Gilbert's of Churchill, and histories such as Will Durant's (Churchill was much influenced by the histories of Macaulay and Gibbon). I have found particularly useful *Viking's Book of Aphorisms* and the *Home Book of Humorous Quotations*, which are divided by subject matter.

I suggest that you start a notebook. I use loose leaf notebooks, but you can also use 3 by 5 cards that can be filed away in boxes. Here are some favorites of mine to start you off with an alphabet of quotations by topic.

ACTION

The Maxim "Perfection" often spells paralysis.

—WINSTON CHURCHILL

BUSINESS

Every great man of business has got somewhere a touch of the idealist in him.

—WOODROW WILSON

CHALLENGE

This time, like all other times, is a very good one, if we but know what to do with it.

—RALPH WALDO EMERSON

DEMOCRACY

Democracy is the worst form of government—except for all those other forms that have been tried from time to time.

—WINSTON CHURCHILL

EXCELLENCE

Ay, but a man's reach should exceed his grasp, Or what's a heaven for?

—ROBERT BROWNING

FREEDOM

Freedom is a good horse but you must ride it somewhere.

—MATTHEW ARNOLD

GOVERNMENT

Any government that is big enough to give you all you want is big enough to take it all away.

—RONALD REAGAN

HISTORY

The further backward we look, the further forward we can see.

—WINSTON CHURCHILL

IDEAS

A new and valid idea is worth more than a regiment and fewer men can furnish the former and command the latter.

—Justice OLIVER WENDELL HOLMES

JUSTICE

Whenever a separation is made between liberty and justice, neither, in my opinion, is safe.

—EDMUND BURKE

KNOWLEDGE

I keep six honest serving-men
  (They taught me all I knew);
  Their names are What and Why and When
  And How and Where and Who.

—RUDYARD KIPLING

LAW

Not every defeat of authority is a gain for individual freedom nor every judicial rescue of a convict a victory for liberty.

—JUSTICE ROBERT JACKSON

MATERIALISM

Things are in the saddle,
 And ride mankind.

—RALPH WALDO EMERSON

NEWSPAPERS

I hope we never have to see the day when a thing is as bad as some of our newspapers make it.

—WILL ROGERS

OPPORTUNITIES

A man must make his opportunity, as oft as find it.

—FRANCIS BACON

POLITICS

History is past politics, and current events present history.

—WOODROW WILSON

QUESTION

Judge a man by his question rather than by his answers.

—VOLTAIRE

RESPONSIBILITY

The price of greatness is responsibility.

—WINSTON CHURCHILL

SOLUTION

I am interested in the next step not the two-hundredth.

—THEODORE ROOSEVELT

TECHNOLOGY

Unless the intellect of a nation keeps abreast of all material improvements, the society in which that occurs is no longer progressing.

—WINSTON CHURCHILL

UNIVERSITY

Men must be born free; they cannot be born wise, and it is the duty of the university to make free men wise.

—ADLAI STEVENSON

VOCATION

I . . . beseech you that ye walk worthy of the vocation wherewith ye are called.

—APOSTLE PAUL

WELFARE

If you give a man a fish, he will have a single meal. If you teach him how to fish, he will eat all his life.

—KUAN-TZU (CHUANG-TSE)

YOUTH

Give me the young man who has brains enough to make a fool of himself.

—Robert Louis Stevenson

ZEAL

No folly is more costly than the folly of intolerant idealism.

—WINSTON CHURCHILL

Now that you have a skeletal structure to begin your own quote file, you can collect and add your own. New topics will come to you as you read the newspaper or the weekly news magazine. Some of these might need new topic labels such as "Bureaucracy," "Economy," "Cost," or "Preparedness." The *New York Times* and *Wall Street Journal* feature one quotation each day. *Forbes* magazine regularly offers a selection of crisp and apt quotations.

If you have only one (or possibly just) two quotations in your speech, don't just read it, flaunt it. Take the 3 by 5 card with you to the speech, and make a show of pulling it out of your breast pocket at the designated time. Little theatrics such as flashing a quotation card not only dramatize your quotation but also deliver a change of pace in the tempo of your talk. Often you will find on the day you are giving your talk, or the day before, an editorial, column or news story that exactly illustrated the theme of your talk. Clip the story or column and put it in you wallet or breast pocket to pull out at the strategic time.

Quote-Noting

Have you ever had your interest aroused by a quotation but then left mildly unsatisfied? Sometimes just the author followed by a quotation is not enough. For example, George Washington said, "To be prepared for war is one of the most effectual means of preserving peace." The sophisticated listener is curious to find out when George Washington said it or where or under what circumstances.

The audience would enjoy this introduction of the Washington quotation.

> The new constitution gave the thirteen states a strong government but the country was still threatened by the British in Canada to the North and to the South were the French in Louisiana. President Washington was worried that the Americans could find themselves entangled in the hostilities between these two great European powers. In his first address to Congress he urged strengthening the national defenses. The old General said that only strength could insure peace. "To be prepared for war is one of the most effectual means of preserving peace."

I call this fleshing out of a quotation *quote-noting*. One ideal place for *quote-noting* is when too familiar a quotation is used.

For example, you might say in a speech, "Charles Dickens once said, 'It was the best of times, it was the worst of times.' . . ."

How much better to begin this way:

> A great English author struggled for the right way to begin his novel about the late eighteenth century, a time when the forces of wealth and poverty, repression and reform, superstition and enlightenment were clashing. At last Charles Dickens wrote the opening words of *A Tale of Two Cities* : "It was the best of times," . . .

By this technique you make the audience try to guess the quotation before you deliver it. If you can make two or three listeners nudge their neighbor and say, "It's Dickens— 'the best of times and worst of times,' " you have the listener hooked. Try out the way I have introduced the quotation to some friends. They will not all identify the Dickens quotation at the same time. Those who quickly guess it will think better of themselves and the speech. Making some of the audience feel good is one technique of speech persuasion and entertainment.

I follow a simple rule about using too familiar or trite quotations. It is permissible and even entertaining as long as you tell the audience something about the quotation they never knew before.

Billy Herndon, Lincoln's law partner, heard Theodore Parker preach in Boston in 1854. He sent the sermon to Lincoln underlining Parker's superbly stated definition of democracy: "government of the people, and by the people." Lincoln would adapt that line in his famous concluding sentence of the Gettysburg address, "that government of the people, by the people and for the people shall not perish from the earth."

Or consider this *quote-noting* :

> In a well known Shakespeare play a character receives a note that reads: "Be not afraid of greatness. Some are

> born great, some achieve greatness, and some have greatness thrust upon them." Shakespeare's Malvolio in *Twelfth Night* is not the only one who has greatness thrust upon him.

Shakespeare's quotations are often familiar even though the authorship is not immediately recognized. "All difficulties are easy when they are known." You follow the quotation by adding that what Shakespeare's Duke of Vienna said in his play, *Measure for Measure*, applies to us today.

If a quotation from Shakespeare, the Bible, or Abraham Lincoln is well known, look it up and try to give the audience interesting background on the quotation.

> Three and a half millennia ago a young shepherd in Judea prophesied to his fellow Israelites. The prophet Joel preached, "Your old men shall dream dreams, your young men shall see visions."

> Do you know the place in the Scripture the Bible is most opened to when Presidents (not to mention governors) take their oath of office? It is Micah, Chapter 6, verse 8. "What doth the Lord require of thee, but to do justly, and to love mercy and to walk humbly with thy God?" A young shepherd wrote this canon of responsibility thousands of years ago, but it applies just as aptly to us today.

Sometimes it is fun to correct a common misconception of a quotation:

> We often hear the old saying "Money is the root of all evil." But that is not what the Apostle Paul wrote to Timothy, his young protégé; what he said was, "The *love* of money is the root of all evil."

Another Biblical quotation that I like to explain to audiences is the Beatitude, "Blessed are the meek for they shall inherit the earth." "Meek" is the wrong word if it conveys the sense of "docile" or "passive." The original Greek word is *praos* with one meaning being "willing to accept training," or even "ready to accept the discipline of education."

Get into the habit of *quote-noting*. Look up a quotation and find out when and where the author said it. How old was he and in what period of his life? What was happening in his immediate world?

I looked up Patrick Henry's quotation, "I have but one lamp by which my feet are guided and that is the lamp of experience. I know no way of judging the future but by the past." It was uttered at the same time he said, "Give me liberty or give me death" at St. John's Church in Richmond in 1775.

There are many useful quotations from a certain Frenchman that are worth collecting. Here is a way several of them can be introduced:

> A great philosopher came to this country from France in the early nineteenth century to discover what made our democracy work and what was the secret of our success. And Alexis de Tocqueville wrote:
>
> "If I were asked to what the singular prosperity and growing strength of that people ought mainly to be attributed I should reply, 'It is the superiority of their women.'..."
>
> "The greatness of America lies in her ability to repair her own faults."

Alexander Hamilton once said, "Energy in the executive is the leading character in the definition of good government." I found the source was the *Federalist Papers* which Hamilton, John Jay, and James Madison published under pseudonyms to arouse support for ratifying the new Constitution.

In a speech I was writing for a head of a corporation, I was told the talk was to be mostly centered on a summary of the past three years in growth and profits. I thought of the Shakespeare quotation "What is past is prologue." Then I remembered that the conference which the corporation executive was to address was to be held in Bermuda. Something struck a bell. Didn't that quotation come from *The Tempest*? And wasn't *The Tempest* written by Shakespeare after he heard of a shipwreck in what is now Bermuda? I was right, and once again q*uote-noting* proved to be a fruitful exercise.

Quotations in a speech wake people up. The mind of the audience snaps to attention as a great name is heard. Like expert testimony, the right quotation helps persuade the unpersuaded and convince the unconvinced.

Cross-Quotesmanship

If your speech is going to advance a certain political proposal, the best way to sell it to your audience is to use the technique of *cross-quotesmanship*.

Cross-quotesmanship is the citing of liberals to prove the merit of conservative proposals, and vice versa. Conservatives who are against big government quote a hero of liberals, Woodrow Wilson. "The history of liberty is the limitation of governmental power not the increase of it." On the other hand, liberals fearful of the Pentagon's growing power cite former President Dwight D. Eisenhower's warning on defense spending, "In the councils of government, we must guard against the acquisition of unwarranted influence, whether sought or unsought, by the military industrial complex."

When Arthur Schlesinger, Jr., was attacked as a socialist for supporting the welfare state, he replied by quoting Robert Taft's statements in favor of public housing. At the other end of the spectrum, Victor Lasky used anti-Kennedy quotes from the same Arthur Schlesinger, Jr., as well as from Eleanor Roosevelt to puncture the liberal record of Senator John Kennedy in his book, *J.F.K.: The Man and the Myth*.

In 1970, on behalf of the State Department, I quoted Robert Kennedy in support of bombing of Communist bases in Indo-China.

At the same time in the Senate, a staff counsel named Bob Smith helped prevent two major pieces of legislation with the uses of cross-quotes. To defeat the direct-election bill, he made available to the Senators opposing it a list of critical statements by such authorities as former Attorney General Nicholas Katzenbach, author Theodore White, and John F. Kennedy.

And in beating down the Equal Rights Amendment, Smith fed to the Senators critical remarks from such certified liberals as Cesar Chavez, Eleanor Roosevelt and Margaret Mead. As Bob Smith told his boss Sam Ervin at the time of the fight, "These quotes give us credibility, Senator."

The Carter White House paraded statements of John Wayne to prove that the Panama Treaty giving the Canal back to the Panamanians was right. Today the Reagan White House features statements by Democratic Senators Bradley and Nunn as well as former Governor Robb of Virginia to generate support for aid to the Contras in Nicaragua.

We live today in sort of a McLuhanesque world where the fact of a person saying something is more important than what he says. The magazines *Human Events* and *National Review* on the right are fertile sources for *cross-quotes*. On the left *New York Review of Books* and *Village Voice* provide rich material. Journals on the far side of the spectrum often reserve their bitterest denunciation for politicians presumably of their own stripe who stray from the accepted line.

In a persuasive argument, an attack on business holds more credibility if delivered by a businessman. A broadside against welfare policies or affirmative action holds more weight if a black economist like Thomas Sowell or a black journalist like William Raspberry is cited.

When you use a cross-quote, remember to put it on a card and brandish it when you read it. *Cross-quotesmanship* is the most effective and enjoyable use of quotations.

Chapter 9

Mind-Wakers
and Mini-Plays

I deal with four agents who book me speeches all over the country. In the last ten years the only state to which I have not traveled to give a paid lecture is Alaska. The only criticism passed on to me by these agents from the program chairman is that I did not speak long enough! Can you imagine? Some have actually complained that I spoke for fifty or fifty-five minutes instead of the contracted one hour.

Actually I advise those in my communication seminars never to speak beyond twenty minutes. I tell them, "If you don't strike oil in twenty minutes, stop boring!" But I am a professional speaker. Organizations in California don't pay me to fly all across the country to speak for a short time. They want their money's worth, which includes forking out a handsome fee plus air travel and hotel room. So I am under pressure to deliver the goods. After all I'm not a household name whose face is instantly recognized from frequent appearances or television, or having my picture in *People* magazine.

If a celebrity fails to deliver a good speech, it is the celebrity's fault, not the program chairman's. But if I fail, the program chairman gets the blame. After all it is enough just to see and shake hands with Charlton Heston—they are so inspired by just looking at him they don't have to learn anything. But the noncelebrity speaker has to be entertaining as well as enlightening. It is not enough just to be amusing. Audiences don't want a Chocolate Sundae speech. They might enjoy the rich concoction as they eat it, but afterward they feel that they got calories without content. They got fat without getting real food. In the same way if I just was entertaining and amusing, the audience might enjoy me as I spoke but afterward feel a little cheated by learning nothing substantial.

Do you know why readers flock to buy the latest James Michener book? Because they learn about Hawaii, South Africa, or Texas while being entertained by a plot filled with romance and adventure. When they finish, they have not only enjoyed a good yarn but they also have been educated by gaining some rich historical and anthropological insights.

Mind-Wakers

A speaker must be interesting as well as instructive. Authoritative quotations and illustrative anecdotes are *mind-wakers*. They not only brighten your message but also break the monotonous pace of your oral delivery.

In the dining room of a national chain hotel I found

73

myself eating dinner one night while on a lecture tour because the rainy weather discouraged me from going outside. In the midst of the meal, the waiter brought a foot-tall glass filled mostly with cracked ice, with a bit of sherbet and a strawberry on top of that.

The waiter pontificated in a fake French accent, "This is your palate refreshener."

Well, sometimes in a speech we need an ear refreshener, a *mind-waker*. *Mind-wakers* not only waken the mind of the audience but sometimes yourself. *Mind-wakers* include quotations, illustrative anecdotes of well-known personalities, and your own personal experiences. Mind-wakers are snappy quotations or colorful anecdotes that offer a change of pace in the speaker's delivery and perk up attention. Two of my favorite types of *mind-wakers* are *Alice-in-Wonderlands* and *Contemporary Antiquities*.

Alice-in-Wonderlands

One *Alice-in-Wonderland* that fits into almost every speech is this:

> We remember that the Queen says to Alice in *Through the Looking Glass* "It takes all the running you can do to keep in the same place."

Or if you are talking about a problem that is mounting rapidly each day, you might want to repeat what the White Queen once said to Alice.

> "What's one and one and one and one and one and one and one and one and one and one?" asks the Queen, and Alice replies, "I don't know, I lost count."

To outline a vision for the future you might want to quote the same White Queen:

> "It's a poor memory that only works backward."

Or in discussing a definition of goals, you can quote the exchange between the Cheshire Cat and Alice.

> She asks: "Would you tell me, please, which way I ought to walk from here?"
>
> "That depends a good deal on where you want to get to," said the Cat.

Contemporary Antiquities

The best crowd pleaser of the *mind-wakers* is the *contemporary antiquity*. In one speech I said:

> Recently I read an editorial which said, "Society is deteriorating. Bribery and corruption abound. Children no longer mind their parents and every man thinks he has a book or story to tell and it is clear that the collapse or end of the world is at hand."

I paused for a beat and then added, "Such was the warning inscribed on a tablet in Assyria around 3000 B.C."

Another contemporary antiquity could be set up this way:

> Recently some words of an influential Boston politician came to my attention: "Many thinking people believe America has seen its best days." Those words were written to his wife by James Allen, a delegate to the Continental Congress in Philadelphia in July 1775.

For President Ford I used this piece in the Bicentennial year of 1976:

I note the words of one editorial entitled "Why Should We Have a National Birthday?" "We have just come through a divisive war. Our army with superior numbers and weaponry has been defeated by ill-equipped bands. Members of a recent presidential administration have been indicted for acts of corruption and malfeasance in office. Crime in our cities is increasing at an all time rate." This was the editorial of the New York *Tribune* in 1876 when in the aftermath of the Civil War General Custer and his troops were wiped out in the battle of Little Bighorn. Members of the Grant Administration had gone to jail, and crime, because of the influx of immigration, had risen to an all-time high.

A very relevant *contemporary antiquity* goes as follows:

"Our teenagers love luxury. They have bad manners, contempt for authority, they show disrespect for their parents, they mock them at home and tyrannize their teachers at school."

I have heard more than one speaker preface this quotation by saying, "Plato once wrote. . . . " But the entertainment comes in making the audience believe you are reading a contemporary editorial. Then you pause and tell them that was what Plato wrote some 2,400 years ago.

Another favorite contemporary antiquity of mine goes like this:

I read where a southern politician wrote about bureaucracy in administration: "He has erected a multitude of New Offices and sent other swarms of Officers to harass our people and eat out their substance." Well, that's what Thomas Jefferson wrote in the Declaration of Independence.

A relative of the contemporary antiquity is "date-mating." If your speech focuses on a date in history, find out what also happened in that year. In 1959 I was asked to deliver a talk honoring an organization's centennial. After some research I learned that *Uncle Tom's Cabin* by Stowe, *Civil Disobedience* by Thoreau, *Das Kapital* by Marx among many other things were all published in 1859.

The Illustrative Anecdote

Another kind of *mind-waker* is the illustrative anecdote. These can provide bridges or transitions to your speech. For example, if you are discussing possible solutions to a problem, you might want to quote the dying words of Gertrude Stein as recalled by Alice B. Toklas:

> At first she murmured, "What is the answer? What is the answer?" Then after a long silence, she said, "No, what is the question?"

This is an effective *mind-waker* to use when a speaker wants to redefine a problem.

If you want to comment on how ideals sometimes sound like platitudes you may want to use this vignette:

> At the 1875 centennial observance of the Battle of Concord, Ralph Waldo Emerson was invited to deliver the address. He spoke on America and the message of freedom that affirms hope to peoples everywhere. Afterward Rufus Choate, the politician, dismissed the talk to Carl Schurz, who was sitting next to him, saying, "It was full of glittering generalities." Schurz, the immigrant from Bismarck's Germany and a friend of Lincoln, said, "You're wrong—it was full of blazing

ubiquities—meaningful then and now, here and everywhere."

If you are discussing the need to assume responsibility, you might want to use this scriptural tale:

> We remember reading the Bible of King Belshazzar's Feast. When the man's hand wrote on the wall of the palace these words: *Mene, mene, tekel, upharsin.* (You have been counted, you have been weighed, and you have been found wanting.)

A *mind-waker* I find useful either to begin a talk or as a bridge is this.

> The Chinese word for crisis is *wo-jei*. It is composed of two pictographic characters joined together [here the speaker holds up his left hand—fingers half closed facing out suggesting a Chinese letter], the word for "danger" and next to it the word for "opportunity" [here the speaker holds up the right hand in the same way next to it]. "Danger" and "opportunity." Well we have a danger facing us but we also have a unique opportunity. . . .

Another *mind-waker* with a Chinese background is this story, which is a useful bridge or speech continuer when your creative juices are blocked:

> Thousands of years ago a Chinese emperor calledh i s family's most trusted adviser to the throne in the Forbidden City. "O learned counselor," said the emperor, "you have advised my father and grandfather. What is the single most important advice you can give me to rule my country?" And Confucius replied, "The first thing you must do is define the problem."

78

The Mini-Play

Besides the *mind-waker* another speech tonic is the *mini-play*. The *mini-play* is an exchange of conversation from your own experience which pumps a speech with new life.

In one of my Wharton seminars, a municipal executive was delivering a talk on the Philadelphia city charter, which established ground rules for the civil service. In his talk he said, "The reform administration of Mayor Joseph Clark took the personnel process out of the hands of the ward leaders, and so new guidelines had to be issued to set up criteria for hiring."

In my critique I told him that the talk at that point called for a mini-play. For example, he might have said:

> In the old days a guy used to come into the personnel office and say, "Big Red from the 10th Ward sent me and said I could get a job."
>
> And the officer replied, "Well, what is your background—what is your expertise?"
>
> "What do you mean, what's my ex-per-tise—I delivered the 21st Division. Just ask Big Red."

This kind of mini-play, even if imaginary, puts color into your talk. You might try imitating the gruff accent of the job seeker. If you do that, you have a spectacular *mini-play* that will delight your audience.

I heard a woman deliver a talk about sexism in the office, detailing practices such as a male sending a female executive out for coffee, telling her to take something to the cleaners, or asking her to pick out an anniversary card for his wife.

Again this talk cried out for a mini-play. She could have said in a low voice to simulate that of her boss, "Dear, would you be a sweetheart? When you're out for lunch, look in at the card shop and pick out a card for my wife—I just remembered, it's my wedding anniversary."

I remember what a black taxi driver named Fish told me in the West Indies island of Antigua shortly after the liberation of Grenada. I said, "Mr. Fish, what did you think of the situation in Grenada?"

He replied, "Mr. Humes, I be poor and free. Under Communism, I be poor and not free."

Look over the text of your own speech and see if an opportunity does not present itself for inserting a *mini-play* by recasting expository language into conversational exchange. Obviously if you are not Italian or Jewish, you should not imitate an Italian or Jewish accent. Yet if you studied French in school or lived in the south, you may think of incidents in which you develop your own mini-play. It might be as wide ranging as advice a teacher gave you in grade school or what the tour guide in Paris said in his French accent.

Chapter 10

How to Boost Yourself Without Boasting

Some years ago at a Georgetown dinner party, a veteran of the Nixon days was holding forth to listeners about how he told Dick to say this or when he advised Henry Kissenger to do that, when a gentleman at the other end of the table quietly excused himself. When he reappeared, he was seen bending with a small brush and dustpan.

The former functionary, finding that the attention to his continuing account had been diverted to the old gentleman's activity, said, "What are you doing there?"

"Oh, don't mind me," replied the man, "go right ahead. I'm just sweeping up the dropped names."

Audiences find name-droppers a bore, but on the other hand the same listeners want to believe their speaker is an expert who is respected by the peers in his field and has ready access to the powerful, or else they are wasting their time listening to him. Churchill once said of his Labourite successor Clement Atlee, "He is a modest man—with a great deal to be modest about." If a speaker is disinclined to mention names for fear of looking pompous, the audience might go away thinking he didn't have the proper credentials.

Remember the old saying, "Shake the hand that shook the hand of John L. Sullivan"? The speaker's fame rubs off on the audience. It is their link to history and fame. Some may sneer at the pompous, but they all admire power. Mentioning your access to the powerful not only reinforces your authority but elevates the audience. Not o refer to your association with the great is to renounce an important tool in triggering audience interest. Why do you think Time-Life came out with their magazine *People* some decades ago? Because they found that the "people" section in T*ime* was the most widely read part.

Negative Name-Dropping

My advice to speakers is to drag in every famous name they can but only if they can do it with a light touch. I call this technique *negative name-dropping*.

Have you ever seen the starlet on the Johnny Carson show? She regales the audience how when she had Julia Child over for dinner, she burned the roast. The key fact is that she counts Julia Child as a friend. Yet she softens the "name-drop" with a neat, self-deprecating touch.

I tell audiences a story that happened in 1956 when I was a volunteer worker at a big Republican dinner where President Eisenhower was the featured speaker.

Just before the dinner started, one of the Secret Servicemen spotted my lapel badge saying "Committee" and said, "Where's the men's room? The President has a call of nature." In the huge arena where the banquet was being held, there were two rest rooms one at each side of the hall. The problem was that I couldn't remember which was which. Yet I was supposed to know, so I pointed to the right and said that way. Then I rushed down the corridor to see if I was right. To my dismay I had chosen wrong. At the door of the lavatory I announced in stentorian tones "Everybody out! Everybody out! Emergency! President of the United States!" Some distressed GOP dowager was flushed out like a ruffed grouse. I immediately turned the door back to hide the telltale sign just as I spied the President rounding the turn in the corridor. I saluted as the President entered, and then I closed the door. Minutes later the President, who must have noticed rather different equipment than he was used to seeing, exited. His steel-blue eyes drilled holes in me—eyes fueled by a general's distaste of sloppy staffwork. Eisenhower, who ran a very tight ship at the White House, had a maxim: "There should be no emergencies, only contingencies." I had failed to see the contingencies.

Another story I tell is about a speech I had a hand in writing that made history as one of the biggest Reagan bloopers. The 1975 speech, which discussed the Third World, contained that particular phrase in six places. Unfortunately, every time Ronald Reagan came to the phrase, he unaccountably added the word "war," e.g., "We must address the problems of the Third World [sic] war." Naturally those at my table, who knew that I had assisted in preparing the talk, looked at me when the President added the word "war" six different times! I tell this story in my talk "Confessions of a White House Ghost." My warning to the audience is that a speaker should never publicly read a text that he hasn't read out loud first in the privacy of his own office or home.

As a lawyer I can tell you that *negative name-dropping*

is akin to the Declaration Against Interest (the opposite of a self-serving statement, an exception to the credential Hearsay Rule). In short, a story that puts one in a bad light has credibility because it is presumed that the teller would not tell a story against himself.

In Washington, aides often use the n*egative name-drop* to advance their own access to power; e.g., "George Schultz bawled me out for my memo." For the price of a small failure he purchases fame and announces his access to power.

Global Gamesmanship

A variation of negative name-dropping is *place name-dropping,* or *global-gamesmanship.* In 1960 while working for Vice President Nixon, I wanted to give an opportunity to Nixon to proclaim his foreign policy experience. Nixon could not just say in a speech, "I'm experienced." We had to bring in experience in an indirect way. So I wrote down a list of all the famous world leaders Nixon had met in his travels as Vice President: Churchill, Adenauer, De Gasperi, DeGaulle, Tito, Ben-Gurion. Then I read biographies of leaders to collect quotations of them that could be used in speeches.

So Nixon would say, "I remember meeting Prime Minister Nehru in New Delhi in 1959, and one of Nehru's favorite sayings is, 'What the world needs is a generation of peace.' " Nixon probably did not actually hear Nehru say that. But the quotation gave Nixon the opportunity to mention his meeting with Nehru in a foreign capital of the world.

Similarly, I would suggest you make a list of every famous person you have come in contact with or have some association with. Perhaps someone famous was born in your home town or attended your high school. Look up a biography or magazine articles in your library, and see if you can find one apt quotation or anecdote that you can put to constructive use in your speech.

For a governor who was an officer in the South Pacific under Admiral Halsey, I had him say, "It was my privilege to serve under Admiral Halsey. They called him the Bull. He used to say, 'You're never down til you're dead.' "

For a Congressman who was running for the Senate, I made use of the fact that he had traveled to China as well as Germany and Israel.

> In the last few years I have seen three walls. The Berlin Wall erected to prevent seekers of freedom from leaving tyranny, the Great Wall of China that was built to prevent invasion, and the Wailing Wall in Jerusalem which is a monument to man's fight for dignity under God against oppression by man.

Perhaps the speaker wants to mention that recently he testified at a Congressional hearing. He might say:

> Some time ago I was in Washington where I was testifying to a Congressional Committee. The cab took me from my hotel past the White House on Pennsylvania Avenue to the Capitol. I recalled then the story recounted in Carl Sandburg's biography of Lincoln when Congressman Ben Wade stormed into Lincoln's office at the White House saying, "Mr. President, this administration is going straight to Hell. In fact, Mr. President, it's only about a mile from there right now!"
>
> "Why, Ben," replied Lincoln, "isn't that the distance from the White House to the Capitol?"
>
> Similarly, with the way Congress is pushing for protectionism right now—we're heading for the fires of overheated inflation. . . .

If you or the person you are writing a speech for has ever been to the White House with a group to meet the President, you might want to allude to the fact this way:

> The other week when I was at the White House for a meeting, I noticed a painting just outside the Oval Office. I took a second look at it because it's a peculiar portrait—only about a fourth completed, with the rest stark gray canvas with only a few lines penciled in. It is titled, "Signing of the Declaration." I asked about it, and I was told that President Eisenhower had discovered it in the catacombs of the White House and had it hung because he thought it manifested the hand of Divine Providence. The artist who had been commissioned by Congress to paint it died before he could complete it. But Eisenhower thought that perhaps the message was that it is not just the Signers who had the obligation to preserve those freedoms but all of us. There is a place in that canvas for all of us. All of us can be signers of that Declaration.

Such a story not only drops the name of a place (the White House) but also, by implication, the name of President Reagan you had your appointment with.

In today's world many of us travel more in a year than our grandparents did in a lifetime. Reference to that travel in a talk can suggest to an audience that the speaker has a broad, cosmopolitan, and fascinating background. So I have listed by country or region some speech brighteners that you can weave into the context of your speech.

AUSTRIA

In Salzburg I learned this story about Mozart. A young composer came to him for advice on how to develop his talents.

He answered, "Begin writing simple things first. Write songs for example." The man countered, "But you wrote symphonies when you were only a child." "Oh," Mozart answered, "but I didn't go to anybody to find out how to become a composer." I use this story to show that creativity—be it in the artist, statesman, or entrepreneur—cannot be taught.

BOLIVIA

Bolivia, of course, is named for its liberator, Simon Bolivar—the George Washington of South America. In 1820 Bolivar was asked how long the struggle would take to rid the country from Spanish rule. He answered, "We are seeing the light now, and it shall not be our destiny to be thrust back into the darkness." I have used this to introduce progress that has been made or the first steps that have been taken.

CANADA

While in Quebec, I saw the Plains of Abraham to which General Wolfe ascended for his surprise attack against the French in 1759. As Wolfe was rowed up the St. Lawrence River, he recited aloud the words of Gray's "Elegy in a Country Churchyard" whose most poignant words end "The boast of heraldry, the pomp of pow'r/And all that beauty, all that wealth e'er gave/Await alike the inevitable hour:/The paths of glory lead but to the grave." It was prophetically true in Wolfe's case. The victor did not survive the battle. In a talk to an arts group you might want to tell this to emphasize the endurance of artistic triumphs.

CHINA

There is an old Chinese proverb: If a bird drops a deposit on your head, that you cannot prevent. But if he builds a nest in your hair, that you can. This can be used in a discussion of planning.

ENGLAND

While in London, I visited St. Paul's Cathedral, that splendid edifice which inspired our own Capitol and was the scene of Prince Charles's marriage as well as Churchill's funeral. When the architect Christopher When completed the Cathedral in 1706, there was a dedicatory service which Queen Anne attended. After the service the Queen told Wren, "I find the Cathedral awful, artificial, and amusing." Wren replied, "Your majesty, I am flattered by your words." Actually at that time "awful" meant majestic, "artificial" meant artistically made, and "amusing" meant amazing! I tell this story to emphasize the problem of changed circumstances.

FRANCE

There is a plaque in the lobby of the Hotel de Crillon in Paris. The reason for the plaque goes back to 1589 when King Henry IV of France won a bloody victory at Arques while his erstwhile friend and supporter Crillon stayed away. The message that Henry IV supposedly sent Crillon is now emblazoned on the hotel wall. "Hang yourself brave Crillon! We have fought at Arques, and you were not there." Use this story to ask for involvement and participation.

GREECE

In ancient Athens everyone was expected to participate in civic life and take an interest in government. They had a word for a businessman who did not involve himself in public life. The word was 'idiot.' [A great story for a business audience]

HUNGARY

While in Budapest, I passed by the home of Ferenc Molnar, the great Hungarian playwright. I learned the story of an occasion when Molnar and his lady friend were offered two tickets to a play. Early in the insufferable first act Molnar got up to leave. "You can't walk out," objected his companion. "We're guests of the management." Molnar meekly sat down, but after a few more doses of insipid dialogue, he rose again. "Now where are you going?" asked his friend. Replied Molnar, "I'm going to the box office to buy some tickets so we can leave." I have used this talk about the need, even if expensive, to extricate one from a difficulty.

INDIA

In Calcutta I learned of the first time Buddha went from his father's estate to visit that city. He saw a leper and asked his driver," What is that?" The reply was, "Think nothing of it, Master, that is the way of life." Next he saw a blind man begging for alms and again to his question came, "Think nothing of it, Master, that is the way of life."

And finally he saw a corpse lying in the road being consumed by flies and vultures. Again the driver's answer was, "Think nothing of it, Master, that is the way of life." But Buddha said, "No, that must not be the way of life." It was then that he started on his life of service. I have related to this story to many voluntary action groups.

ISRAEL

I heard the story recounted of when Dr. Chaim Weizmann visited President Truman in 1948. Truman said, "Do you know what it's like being President of 180 million people?" Chaim Weizmann replied, "Do you know what it's like being President of a half a million little Presidents?" I have told this anecdote to discuss the problem of divisiveness or factionalism.

ITALY

In Rome you see the route where victorious Roman generals with their armies were given the privilege of a glorious procession through the city. Leading the procession was the general in his magnificent chariot, accepting the ovations of the multitude. But by law it was required that one man be designated to ride in the same chariot with the general, whose only responsibility was to keep whispering in the general's ear, "You're only a man—You're only a man." They did not want the victor to think he was a god.

Sometimes after a flattering introduction I tell this story, and then I add, "Of course, those who have wives don't need that man in the chariot."

JAPAN

While in Japan I learned from some Japanese business associates the Japanese words *wari kiru*. It means cutting through a problem to the core.

Former Senator Howard Baker used *wari kuri* in the Watergate hearings when he asked, "What did President Nixon know and when?"

MEXICO

In my last trip to Mexico I learned that at the jail in Alamos they used to have a regulation providing that a guard must serve out the sentence of any prisoner who escaped while he was on duty. I have used this example to ask audiences, "What if this was applied to judges who give suspended sentences to muggers and rapists who then repeat their crimes?"

PHILIPPINES

In the island of Cebu I came across the monument to Ferdinand Magellan, the Spanish explorer who was killed on that island. He was speared not because he invaded that island but rather because he took sides in a local fight between two tribes. This story is useful for warning people not to get involved in disputes in which they have no first hand knowledge.

POLAND

When I was in Warsaw, I heard several times the Polish proverb that "A guest sees more in an hour than the host sees in a year." This is another way of saying you are too close to the trees to see the forest.

SPAIN

In Madrid you see the relics of Queen Isabella, Spain's greatest Queen. The motto on her coat of arms was *Ne Plus Ultra*, meaning "Nothing Further," which described Spain's geographic position, jutting out into the Atlantic Ocean. But when Christopher Columbus returned and reported his findings, Isabella had the old motto repainted—the *Ne* was removed. It now read *Plus Ultra*—

"something further." I have used this historical vignette to introduce new opportunities.

U.S.S.R.

In struggling with my interpreter in the Soviet Union, I learned a curious fact about their language. The word for "peace" and "world" is the same—*mir*. Sometimes the actions and designs of the Kremlin make one think that their conception of peace is their control of the world. This is ideal for a talk on foreign policy and Soviet paranoia.

In all these g*lobal-gamesmanship* items there is a lesson to drawn or a point to be made. It could be apathy in the Greek word *idiotes*, or opportunity in the motto of Isabella. You should see how you could adopt that foreign experience or bit of knowledge to serve the purpose of your speech.

The point in both g*lobal-gamesmanship* and *negative name-dropping* is to brandish your connections or credentials in an interesting way, presenting them in a brightly wrapped package.

Chapter 11

Soul-Shakers
and Speech-Enders

In the 1960 Presidential campaign as John Kennedy delivered remarks at airports and shopping malls, he would look down at the conclusion of his written text to find a drawn picture of a sun or a candle.

His chief speechwriter Ted Sorenson had drawn these symbols to trigger in Kennedy a particular inspirational story out of history.

The sun represented Benjamin Franklin's remarks at the conclusion of the Constitutional Convention in 1787:

At the close of this convention, the delegates filed up to affix their signatures. Benjamin Franklin was among the first, and he had to be helped to the table, and he wept tears of joy as he signed it. As the others signed, the eighty-year-old Benjamin Franklin rose slowly and pointed to the presiding chair of the convention, the back of which showed a sun low on the horizon. Franklin said, "Gentlemen, I have often, in the course of the session . . . looked at that [sun] behind the President without being able to tell whether it was rising or setting: But now at length I have the happiness to know that it is a rising and not a setting sun."

The second of these involved a speaker of the House of Delegates in Connecticut, a Colonel Davenport:

On June 4, 1780, in Hartford, Connecticut, there was an eclipse of the sun so that even at noon it looked like midnight. In that day, more religious than our own, many thought it was the end of the world—that Judgment Day had arrived. In the House of Delegates at Hartford, many frightened legislators in panic motioned for adjournment. The Speaker of the House, Colonel Davenport, voted down the motions and silenced the commotion with these words: "Gentlemen of the House, the Day of Judgment has either come or it has not come. If it has not come, there is no need to adjourn, but if it has come, I want the Lord to find me doing my duty. I, therefore, will entertain the motion that candles be brought into this chamber to enlighten this hall of Democracy."

Each of these closing anecdotes had the inspirational force to bring Kennedy's remarks to an emotional climax. I call such stories *soul-shakers*, which serve as speech-enders, guaranteed to produce sustained applause if not a standing ovation.

I have collected over the years hundreds of these *soul-shakers*. Almost all of these touch on such emotionally charged subjects as God, country, family, or death. Patriotism, religion or deathbed statements can fuse feelings into a powerful climax.

Most of us, when asked to list the most moving address we have heard, will list one of three, and our choice reflects upon our age as well as our political preference. The three are Douglas MacArthur's "Farewell Address," John Kennedy's inaugural, and Martin Luther King's "I Have a Dream."

Memorable eloquence is composed of four elements: great man (or woman), great occasion, great words, and great delivery. If we work hard on a speech and practice, we might achieve the last two criteria. But the first two are beyond our reach. We have not gained eminence and rarely are afforded the great occasion such as addressing Congress like MacArthur, delivering a Presidential inaugural like Kennedy, or speaking to hundreds of thousands of civil rights marchers before Lincoln Memorial like Dr. King.

In my own experience I can think of two occasions where I had the opportunity for eloquence. The first was in 1963 when as a state legislator in Pennsylvania I was asked to give a eulogy for President John Kennedy the day after he was shot. The aged Parliamentarian, Edward Moore, generously sent me a note saying it was the most moving address he had heard since he began his duties in 1908. But to look at it another way, no President had been slain in those sixty-five years (McKinley was killed in 1901). I was handed a unique opportunity, an occasion for stirring emotions that few speakers are given. I used, as a closer, the adapted words from the Greek poet Simonides found carved in the rocks of Thermopylae.

> *Go, passer-by, and to Sparta tell*
> *That they in faithful public service fell.*

The other occasion was in 1985 in Brisbane, Australia, where I was asked to deliver a keynote address to a national party convention. In representing President Reagan before 2,000 delegates I was presented with an occasion, and if I was not a "great man," I was at least surrogate for a great man. I worked hard on my address, fashioning each word and statement of a conservative credo.

I used as a "closer" to stress the ties of English-speaking people the last meeting of Churchill and Eisenhower.

> General Eisenhower in September 1964 had come over for the twentieth anniversary of D-Day and had stopped to see the aging Churchill who was in King George V Hospital. The old Prime Minister, his face flaccid with nine decades of infirmities, suddenly beamed with the recognition of his old friend at the door. His cherubic pink hand reached over to the bedside table to clasp Eisenhower's. No words were spoken—just two old men holding hands—just two men sharing silently the memories of the battles they together fought for the ideals they mutually cherished. Four minutes passed— still no words spoken—only two old men holding hands. No one save Churchill himself could have written words more poignant, more eloquent than that mute hand clasp of two nations, two leaders, and . . . two friends. Fourteen minutes passed, and then Churchill unclasped his hand and gently waved in a vee sign. Eisenhower withdrew from the room and said to one of his family outside, "I just said good-bye to Winston, but you never say farewell to courage."

Such an emotional ending guarantees a warm audience response. I try to use similar *soul-shakers* to end every speech I deliver or write for someone else to give. The speech at the local Rotary Club or Chamber of Commerce may lack the stuff of greatness, but we can borrow from a poignant moment in history to grace our speech with greatness. We may not hold high office or possess a household name. And we may not be given a forum to speak on a monumental occasion or at an historical event. Yet we can still reach the height of eloquence by making sure that our speech ends on a dramatic note. We can do that by borrowing the words of a great man at a poignant moment in his life.

The words of Abraham Lincoln are a rich lode for *soul-shakers*. John Kennedy used to close some of his campaign speeches in 1960 with the farewell remarks of Lincoln as he left Springfield for the last time to begin the rail journey for Washington on February 11, 1861. Lincoln said,

> I now leave, not knowing when or whether ever I may return, with a task before me greater than that which rested upon Washington. Without the assistance of that Divine Being who ever attended him I cannot succeed. With that assistance I cannot fail.

Another Lincoln story is the letter he wrote to Joshua Speed a year earlier. Kennedy also used this in his campaign in 1960.

"I know there is a God. I know he hates injustice. But if there is a place for me, I am ready."

Vice President George Bush used this Lincoln vignette in 1986:

> When Abraham Lincoln left Springfield in February 1861 to go to Washington, one of his first stops on the train was Indianapolis. He arrived near sundown to be greeted by a 21 gun salute. 20,000 people had gathered expecting to hear a speech. Lincoln, however, only said a few words—remarks that would sound the theme he would later express in the Gettysburg Address: "Finally my fellow citizens, I appeal to you to constantly bear in mind that not with the politicians, not with Presidents but with you, the question: 'Shall the liberties of this country be preserved to the latest generations.' "

The question and answer technique is an ideal format for a *soul-shaker*. The curiosity about the answer to the question heightens anticipation and dramatizes the answer. Whitney Young, the black leader who died some decades ago in an African airplane crash, used this to close speeches.

> In Athens, where democracy began, a citizen once asked the historian Thucydides, "When will justice come to Athens?" And Thucydides replied, "Justice will not come to Athens until those who are not exploited are as indignant as those who are."

The *soul-shaker* technique is one that should be particularly noted by journalists who are drafted into speech writing duties. Journalists learn their trade by writing stories by the inverted triangle—the most important things first so that the story can be cut off by the editors at any point to meet space requirements. It works well for newspapers, but not for speeches. I think I was the first White House speech writer whose background was that of speaker rather than that of a writer. I noted that many journalistic converts tended to end their speeches anticlimactically. The *soul-shaker* allows the speech writer to close on a dramatic high.

Ronald Reagan often uses *soul-shakers* to close speeches. One of his favorites he took, I am told, from my book *Instant Eloquence*. I had presented one of his speech writers a copy in 1973 in Los Angeles when my old friend Charles Manatt had hosted a party for me.

> When Governor George Winthrop in 1630 called together his Puritan passengers on the flagship *Arabella* to meet the task of building a new colony, he told them:
> "We must always consider that we shall be as a city upon a hill in the eyes of all people upon us."

During his eulogy for the victims of the 1986 space shuttle disaster Reagan closed with a verse from a moving incident in World War II:

> The church across from the White House is St. John's Episcopal, which I often attend. One of its famous rectors was Reverend John Gillespie Magee, who served there during the second World War. His son and namesake volunteered for the Royal Canadian Air Force in 1941 before we entered the war. He died in a mission over Germany. After his death the rector received a letter from his pilot son, who enclosed a poem. The last three lines are:
>
> *And, while with silent, lifting mind I've trod*
> The high untrespassed sanctity of space,
> Put out my hand and touched the face of God.

Deathbed statements are another rich mine for *soul-shakers* as in this favorite closer by the late Senator Sam Ervin.

> In the Museum of History in Raleigh is displayed one of the most poignant letters in American history. The letter is only one sentence long but the most unusual feature about it is that it is written in—the writer's blood. The writer was Colonel Avery, a confederate cavalry commander who, while dying in action from wounds, took his sword and etched his epitaph in his own blood:
>
> "Tell my father," he wrote, "that I died facing my enemy."

Justice Arlin Adams of Pennsylvania, in a speech to a college, ended with the last words of the educator Horace Mann.

"Be ashamed to die until you have won some victory for humanity."

The Bible is the greatest source of quotations that qualify as *soul-shakers*. Governor Thomas Kean of New Jersey often used the deathbed words of the Apostle Paul.

> In A.D. 67 Apostle Paul found himself jailed by Nero's edict in a Roman prison. The great missionary, now close to death, gave a Christian visitor, Onesiphorus, a message to deliver to his protégé Timothy, who was almost a son to him.
>
> The note declared, "I have fought a good fight, I have finished my course, I have kept the faith."

The prophets, particularly Isaiah, are a good source for *soul-shakers*. The conservative activist Richard Viguerie quoted from Isaiah in this closer.

> To those who say the challenge is too great, the task too hard I remind you what the prophet Isaiah told those who had the same doubts some three thousand years ago: "They that wait upon the Lord shall renew their strength; they shall mount up with wings as eagles; they shall run and not be weary, and they shall walk and not faint."

The best *soul-shaker* is devised by choosing an anecdote or quotation to fit the needs of a particular audience. Sometimes the soul-shaker is regional. When I was a member of the Pennsylvania legislature, which met in Harrisburg on the Susquehanna, I sometimes closed a speech this way:

> In the late eighteenth century English poets planned an artistic colony at the confluence of the two branches of the Susquehanna River. Though the particular plan fell through, the dream continued. And Samuel Taylor Coleridge, whom we know through his poem *Rime of the Ancient Mariner*, wrote another poem which he

delivered as a eulogy at Trinity Chapel in Cambridge University for one of his fellow poets who had died.

> *May we ever follow that sweet dream*
> *Where Susquehanna pours its untamed stream.*

If the quotation does not stir your soul as you read it, remember you are not a resident of the Susquehanna Valley. When a visiting speaker can appeal to local heritage, he has found a potential *soul-shaker*.

Dr. Pat Robertson, the preacher and political leader, closed a speech in a community near Gettysburg with an allusion to its most famous resident.

> In 1969 General Eisenhower, whose roots stemmed from Mennonite preachers from this county of York and who later chose as his home a farm in Gettysburg, lay dying at Water Reed Hospital in Washington.
>
> "Tell them," he said to his wife, "that I have always loved my wife, I have always loved my family, I have always loved my country, I have always loved my God."

John Kennedy in 1960 in Charleston, South Carolina, paid a tribute to one of the South's most famous leaders in history, John C. Calhoun.

> His was a mind that illuminated Washington in the first half of the nineteenth century and his was a voice that never lacked courage and resolution.
>
> When the senior Senator from South Carolina lay dying in his Washington home in the spring of 1850, a friend approached his bedside and said:
>
> "Mr. Calhoun, you are a very unpopular man."
>
> "Yes," replied Calhoun, "I am an unpopular man with the politicians, but not with the people."

Sometimes the best *soul-shakers* come from your own experience.

In 1985 I was speaking at a breakfast in Wilkes-Barre, Pennsylvania, at a political rally.

> I almost did not make the speech today because I was asked if I was available to go to El Salvador as a part of the team to monitor the election. I refused because of my engagement with you.
>
> Before the breakfast a handsome lady with white hair seated in the front row approached me. She was my father's old secretary, who had driven fifty miles to hear me. I have not seen her in forty years. He had a stroke shoveling himself out of snow as he was leaving to deliver a talk. She brought me today his calendar and blotter from that last day. In addition she brought me a book of famous speeches. The book is still open to where he had left it. It was a speech by Benjamin Franklin at the Constitutional Convention. The lines are underlined in red pencil because he was going to quote Franklin in that speech he never got to deliver and I'd like to tell you what the quotation says because it speaks to those who would criticize our government for not always living up to its ideals.
>
> "There are those who would rather have local interests and selfish views. . . . But I consent to this constitution because I expect no better."
>
> And he went on to say that if this new government should ever collapse, it will collapse not because of a failure of what we did but rather because of a failure in what you will do.

Another *soul-shaker* relating to my father's death is another quotation from that speech that he never gave. He was to address a PTA. He closed his talk mentioning a Greek master at the Hill School which he attended as a boy. The teacher had repeatedly drilled into his students the oath Athenians took upon becoming twenty-one.

"We will strive unceasingly to quicken the sense of duty so that we will make this community greater, nobler, and more beautiful than it was when we took this oath."

As a speaker you can ennoble your talk by closing with a *soul-shaker*. Think of the biographies you have read, examine your own life for the poignant experience or research into the history and heritage of the audience or community you are addressing, and you will find the right *soul-shaker*.

Chapter 12

Read a Speech Like Reagan

A *New York Times* article in the fall of 1979 commented on a speech delivered by John Connally. "The former Governor's performance was flat, dull, and uninspiring." The assessment invited inquiry. After all, John Connally is one of the best speakers in America. The times I have seen him both on television and in person, he has projected both a force and a dynamism that few political leaders can match.

The answer was, as I suspected, that he had read his speech. Rare is the leader who has learned how to read speeches in a manner that suggests the direct and intimate nature of a talk given extemporaneously or from a few notes. Yet it is a trick that can be picked up with a little practice of some simple techniques.

Similarly I have heard Lee Iacocca and Congressman Jack Kemp disappoint audiences who expected to be swept off their feet. Both are outstanding speakers when they speak without a text, but they have not learned how to read a speech effectively.

Over the years I have advised many top executives of many leading corporations in America on the problems of oral communication. The chief executive of these firms—some of the biggest banks, insurance companies, oil companies, airlines, and steel and airplane manufacturers in the world—are almost compelled by the scope and sensitivity of their awesome responsibilities to read their speeches. One miscue in an off-the-cuff comment could bring down the angry arm of Uncle Sam in the form of an antitrust regulatory action. A set of prepared remarks by these executives is written by a team of speech writers and then run by the general counsel's office and the vice president for public affairs. When friends and acquaintances of the business leader hear him read the finished product, they are amazed that this executive, whom they find so strong and forceful in private conversation, is so wooden in a public presentation.

In counseling I make it a rule to videotape the chief executive talking informally about his company and the principal problems facing his industry. Then I videotape him reading a well-written speech of current business interest. The comparison is dramatic. When he's conversational, he's dynamic; when he reads, he drones.

Even when the executive tries to put force in his delivery, it sounds more artificial than authoritative. He is speaking at us—not to us. He is not looking at us in the audience. The pace of delivery is both too rapid and too unvaried to seem like the natural flow of conversation.

Words Must Never Leave Your Mouth
While You Are Looking Down At the Text

Photograph a phrase in your eye and then look up and deliver the phrase. Try it once—read aloud portions of a newspaper editorial. Of course, it sounds easier in the print on this page than it is in actual practice. If someone was videotaping you doing it, the replay would show you succeeding in not looking down at first, but then as you approach the end of your "photographed" passage, your eyes would start to look downward to the next piece of text. In other words, at the end of your recital of a phrase, your head is beginning to look down at what follows.

Perhaps you are trying to read the words instead of trying to record a picture of the whole phrase with your eye. You may also be attempting to photograph a whole sentence or too long a phrase.

Don't Photograph Too Long a Phrase
or Sentence

Let your eye record what it can comfortably remember and then look up. Look at this passage from a Churchill speech in 1940:

"However matters may go in France or with the French Government or other French Governments, we in this island and in the British Empire will never lose our sense of comradeship with the French people."

You might choose to break it up like this:

"However matters may go
in France or with the French Government
or other French Governments,

106

we in this island
and in the British Empire
will never lose
our sense of comradeship
with the French people."

Winston Churchill, in fact, broke it up like that and had it so spaced in his typewritten text. Churchill read all of his major speeches—speeches whose impact was so powerful that they helped save a nation on the brink of defeat.

Consider this paradoxical maxim: "Bad speakers read their speeches, good speakers read from notes. Great speakers read their speeches." Good speakers read from an outline or short brief notes. Because they do not read their speech, they maintain some eye contact. The answer to this paradox is that great speakers read their speeches because memorable and quotable lines do not emanate from brief notes. The lines have been carefully crafted. Yet the great speaker knows how to read a speech and still maintain eye contact. The good speaker who looks at notes can keep eye contact, but he fails to come up with the memorable lines. If you don't know how to read a speech, you are advised not to read a text but use brief notes. The great speaker knows that memorable quotable lines do not come off the top of a speaker's head but are products of careful publishing of a prepared text, and the great speaker knows how to read these carefully chiseled lines and yet engage the audience's eyes.

Franklin Roosevelt, Douglas MacArthur, and Ronald Reagan all read their speeches. Reagan cheerfully admits that his model for speaking was Roosevelt, and he copies the "pause" technique that Roosevelt perfected in his fireside addresses.

To read a speech well, you only have to break up sentences in your mind into oral chunks. Churchill called such chunks "snatches"; by that he meant, not phrases that in sum represent an idea or a thought, but a bite-size group of words comfortable to absorb and utter in one breath.

For practice, again select an editorial from the day's paper. True, the piece was not written for the ear. But employing the snatch-snapshot method with dry prose reveals the benefit of this method even more dramatically.

Then, as a way to prevent speaking while you are glancing down or looking up at the page, try this exercise:

1. Look down and eye-photograph.
2. Look up and *pause*.
3. Deliver the phrase and *pause*.
4. Look down and eye-photograph another snatch.
5. Look up and *pause*.
6. Deliver another phrase and *pause*.

Remember the pause is the major tool in reading a speech. It not only helps you to eye-photograph a text phrase by phrase, it helps the audience to digest your words better. The pause just after your words come up from the page makes the audience think you are not reading the speech.

Try the technique out now on an excerpt from Winston Churchill's Iron Curtain speech in 1946:

> A shadow has fallen upon the scenes so lately lighted by the Allied victory. . . .

> From Stettin in the Baltic to Trieste in the Adriatic, an iron curtain has descended across the continent of Europe. Behind that line lie all the capitals of all the ancient

states of Central and Eastern Europe. Warsaw, Berlin, Prague, Vienna, Budapest, Belgrade, Bucharest and Sofia.

Did using the *photograph-pause-deliver-pause* method sound labored, stilted, almost absurd to your ear? Did the pause seem to you artificially jarring? Good! That's the way it always feels at first to the speaker—but not to the listener!

The "pause" may seem like an eternity to a speaker but to the audience it is only a microsecond that "punctuates" the sentence, builds audience anticipation, and helps understanding.

Corporation executives fear the pause is too long when they first practice this method in our session, but when they look at the videotape replay, they are amazed how much it resembles the tempo of their conversational talking style. The halting rhythm and decelerated pacing are a simulation of our normal oral conversational rhythms.

In our conversations we often pause to think of the right word, to organize our thoughts, and to think of the next sentence. We also pause to look at our listener's reaction. The "pause" then is the major difference between a read text and conversation. The pause also forces us to develop a rhythm and to prevent a jerky delivery.

Here is how Churchill gave his speech.

"From Stettin in the Baltic"/pause/

(The audience might not have known exactly where Stettin was, but it associated the Baltic Sea with Northern Europe.)

"to Trieste in the Adriatic"/pause/

(The listeners then connected the Adriatic to Italy and Southern Europe.)

"an iron curtain"/pause/

(Here Churchill gave time for the curtain image to register)

"has descended across the continent of Europe."

In your mind's ear, conjure up the voices of the other great speakers in your lifetime whom you have heard in person, on radio or television or in a recording. Douglas MacArthur, Martin Luther King, Everett Dirkson, and Franklin Roosevelt all read their major speeches. Of course the most vivid current example is Ronald Reagan. Compare the relaxed pacing of a text read by President Reagan to the supercharged delivery of Congressman Jack Kemp.

When I make a speech, I force myself to engage the eyes of my listeners, by sweeping my eyes across the audience in the pattern of a backward squared 2.

I pick someone in the front pew to my left and then move my eyes to the rear. From the center of the back of the hall I work my way up to the front. Then I shift to my right and again move my eyes to the rear of the audience.

It is not necessary to have such a rigid pattern as long as you engage someone's eyes in the audience. Look for that person who seems to be following you intently and then speak to him or her. Then switch your attention to the other side and catch the gaze of someone else.

Of course, you can't do this in the privacy of your study. But for practice, try fixing your eyes on different pieces of furniture. Mount a makeshift podium on your desk by pulling out a drawer and putting it on top. Or by piling up books. Now stand up and read a new editorial passage by the *photograph-pause-deliver-pause* method—setting your eyes on a lamp, then on top of a chair or the rim of a window.

Understandably, speaking to inanimate objects is not the

same as speaking to a live audience. A listener will nod, smile, knit his brow in reflection, or purse his lips in concern.

A speech, just like a conversation, should be a two-way communication, and a speaker must learn to get his cues from such non-oral signs of communication.

When the Nixon tapes were reduced to transcript, some did not make any sense at all. That's because no tapes could record the nods, the shakes of heads, and the other only slightly perceptible body language people convey with their heads, hands, and eyes. A listener can say a lot by turning his eyes upward in disgust or by slamming his fist down in agreement.

The problem in reading a speech without pausing and looking at the audience is that the speaker misses the signals from the audience. He can witness a few nods of assent or maybe the folded arms of skepticism or perhaps too many people looking at their watches.

Always bear in mind that the audience cannot see the copy of the text you are reading—they only hear it. They do not know if you fail to follow the text exactly. If you miss something, pick it up in the next line. If you have to repeat part of a phrase, do it. That only makes it seem more conversational. We repeat parts of phrases when we talk. For example, if you have to read, "Winston Churchill and Franklin D. Roosevelt, the two great political masters of the English language, shared a common mentor and adviser, Bourke Cockran, the American orator." In your first snatch you might say, "Winston Churchill and Franklin D. Roosevelt, the two great political masters of the English language. . . . " And then in your second snatch, pick up "the two great political masters of the English language shared a common mentor and adviser, Bourke Cockran, the

American orator." Even though you are repeating a phrase, don't worry. That is what we often do in conversation.

The pause between snatches not only allows the speaker to read his speech while maintaining eye contact, it allows the audience time to let the words of the speaker sink in and register.

The pauses and broken rhythm of the speaker make it easier to follow. The next time you listen to a speaker at a banquet, check whether he is talking from notes or reading the text. If he is reading, does he pause?

In my experience as a communications consultant, I have found that corporate executives have measurably improved their ability to read speeches just by observing other speakers. They learn why it is necessary to improve their own delivery by noting failure of others to maintain contact with the audience or to control the pace of delivery.

Certain Words Need Special Emphasis

In the English preparatory school I attended before college, the father of one of my classmates was Emlyn Williams, the Welsh playwright and actor who has captivated millions with his readings of Dickens. He told a group of us who were rehearsing for a play, "There is always a key word in every line of dialogue. If you remember and emphasize that word in your line, the others will always have their cue for their own line, even if you don't remember the exact phrasing. So underline the key words as you memorize the script." Williams also said that the way to emphasize a key word is to pause a split second before enunciating it, or sometimes just after uttering it. You don't have to turn up the volume to emphasize a word. The pause introduces and underlines it. While this advice was given to actors, it is helpful for a speaker to know that a split-second pause before or after a word or phrase is the way to emphasize it.

You might want to underline key words or even double-underline, for added emphasis, a word that may be rolled off the tongue with special feeling.

If you want to read a phrase slowly, bracket it in red; for one to be said more quickly, do it in green.

Use a slash / for a slight pause or a double slash // for a longer pause.

If you want to lower your voice, use a downward arrow, and an upward arrow if you want to increase the volume.

"We shall go on till the *end* //. We shall fight in France, we shall *fight* / on the *seas* and *oceans* //, we shall *fight* / with growing *confidence* and growing *strength* in the air/, we shall defend our island, whatever the cost may be, we shall *fight* on the landing grounds //, we shall *fight* in the *fields*/, and in the streets //, we shall *fight* in the hills //; we shall never //*surrender*."

DON'T ASSUME AN ACCENT OR MANNER THAT IS NOT YOUR OWN

A regional or ethnic accent can give you texture and personality. Witness Henry Kissinger with his heavy Teutonic way of speaking or John Kennedy with his Boston Irish or Franklin Roosevelt with his Groton School patrician. When Lyndon Johnson and Jimmy Carter tried to soften their regional accents in television addresses, they lost some of their personality and credibility.

DON'T TRY TO GESTURE, UNLESS IT COMES NATURALLY

Generally those whose ancestors hail from Mediterranean climates gesture more than those from the North. (On the other hand, I seem to gesture as my mother did, although my brothers do not.) The emphasizing gesture of Richard Nixon and George Bush often used to be a split-second off, as if they suddenly remembered their cue to gesture. It would have been better if they had not gestured at all. Churchill, for example, rarely gestured. (At the age of twenty-three, he sustained an arm injury when reaching for a dock in landing in India.)

If you try to change your accent or contrive to gesture, you are going to make mastering the *eye-photograph-pause* technique more difficult. The trick in learning how to read a text like Reagan is not a cerebral one of mental process but rather a mechanical one of eye-hand coordination. The people who pick up this knack most quickly are not the brains but the jocks who have golf or tennis skills. Yet the *eye-photograph-pause* is not difficult to learn—it is no harder than learning to ride a bike.

Do you remember when the golf pro first taught you an overlapping grip? It felt awkward and didn't make much sense to you. In the same way, the "look down to photo-graph—look up—pause—deliver the phrase—pause" method may seem unnatural and artificial. But by practic-ing it, you'll correct that old, ingrained habit of looking down at the page while speaking to an audience, and you'll develop your own comfortable and easy style of talking to an audience instead of talking at them phrases in your text. To read a speech like Reagan you only have to remember this: *Don't ever let words come out of your lips while you are looking down at the lectern!*

114

Chapter 13

How to Use—
and Not Use—Numbers

Benjamin Disraeli once said, "There are three kinds of falsehoods. Lies, damned lies, and statistics."

You have heard the old adage: Figures lie when liars figure. After Thatcher Longstreth ran unsuccessfully for mayor of Philadelphia, he said to the winner, Richardson Dilworth, "Dick, one thing I always admired is the way you could pull those statistics out of your sleeve about housing or jobs to knock down any point I made." Dilworth replied, "Hell, Thatch, I just made them up. I'd think of an odd number with a decimal point and pronounce it as fact."

Winston Churchill once asked the Conservative Party Central Office to provide him with some statistics for a speech. Churchill looked at what they sent to him and called back, "These are no good. I want ones that prove I'm right." When the distressed researcher started to explain that there were no statistics available which exactly proved his argument, Churchill interrupted, "I am not look-ing for revealed truth, I want ammunition. Give me something that sounds right. Even if I'm a bit off, it'll be weeks before they come up with their own statistics that prove I'm wrong, and then I'll throw them some more statistics."

No, most statistics are not concocted. And you should not concoct any because that would jeopardize your au-thority as an expert, which the role of speaker has given. But one or two statistics that fortify your argument can be an invaluable tool, particularly as ammunition for a debate or a question/answer session.

Surveys show that few listeners can remember more than one statistic when leaving the auditorium or banquet hall. The use of three or five clouds the prospects for even one to be remembered.

To make sure your statistics are remembered, follow three rules. I call them the three R's for Reduce, Round Off, and Relate.

Reduce

First, *reduce* the number of statistics you use. If you count seven as you edit your text, cut it to four—or five to three or three to one. If you have two statistics proving the same point, select the one that is the more dramatic.

For example you might say 64 percent of married couples under 30 cannot afford to purchase their own house. You might want to add that 71 percent of those under 28 cannot amass the capital to finance a mortgage. Since the second statistic sounds more alarming, go with it and eliminate the first statistic. To use several statistics to prove the same point confuses more than it confirms.

So cut the number of statistics in a speech by cutting out the duplication.

Round Off

Secondly, you should *round off* the number. Instead of 64 percent you can say, "Almost two out of three." For 21.2 percent, phrase it, "a little over one out of five." Despite the spread of pocket computers, listeners still picture numbers best as extensions of their own hand—two out of five, three out of ten.

Decimal points like 31.8 percent or 72.1 percent might sound as if they are real and not made up. But they are forgotten as soon as they are uttered. Another effective use of numbers is to say, "The sales were tripled" or "unempolyment was cut in half."

Relate

When my father entered Harvard Law School in 1923, Roscoe Pound, the venerable dean, told the first-year students on their first day, "Gentlemen, look to the student on your left. Now look at the student on your right. One of those students you just looked at will not be returning next year."

That grim exercise registered much more impact than saying 32.4 percent will not be coming back for a second year. Dean Pound in that instance "related" a statistic to a picture. He let the audience visualize a statistic. Such a graphic use of numbers etches upon the mind a lasting image.

Years ago in the Eisenhower White House, a speech writer pictured the national debt by saying that if you laid the dollars represented by the national debt end on end, you could go to the moon and back again five times. (Of course, it is even worse today—you could go to the moon and back over fifteen times!)

A mention of 121 million gallons of oil found in a new reserve makes little impact. Relate it instead to a picture by saying that is enough to heat the city of Boston for six winters. You could say there are 80,000 lawyers in the city of Washington. Or you could be more dramatic by saying that there are twice as many lawyers in Washington, D.C., as there are in Japan.

Make stories out of statistics, and they will be remembered. If you give form and flesh to figures, they turn from abstract to solid, from something mathematical to something visual.

So when you read over the first draft of your speech, check every statistic.

Can the number of statistics be *reduced* by eliminating duplication? Can they be *rounded off* to "a handful" or "a little over three out of four" or "almost three out of five"? And finally, can it be *related* to a picture or visual scene?

Chapter 14

The Three Rs of Humor

Do not begin speeches with jokes! That is the most important rule to obey if you do not want to embarrass yourself as a speaker. Too many speakers demean themselves, the credentials they hold, and the title they occupy by retelling some joke they read in the *Reader's Digest* or heard at the country club bar.

Yet repeatedly I am called by CEOs at the last minute saying, "Humes, I need some joke to start off my speech. I know you have a garage full of them."

When I told them that Winston Churchill didn't open his speeches with some joke, they answer, "Well, almost every business leader I hear begins by trying to relax the audience with a joke—so give me one from your files. Anyway, President Reagan tells jokes." And I tell them first that Reagan, who was trained as a professional actor, has developed over the years the polished skills of mimicry and timing. What's more—President Reagan gets laughs because he is the President! The greater the reputation of the speaker, the greater the readiness of the audience to laugh. A celebrity by his prestige and personality can set the stage for comic relief. A poor story by Ronald Reagan or Prince Charles or Henry Kissinger still triggers laughter because it is light relief in a serious if not exalted occasion.

I do not believe in jokes, but I do believe in the use of humor. What's the difference? A joke is just a trick (and a joke that doesn't work plays its trick on the teller). But humor is an attitude—a sign of the speaker's point of view and intent to communicate. In order to use humor correctly, you should follow another Three Rs—your story must be Relevant, Realistic, and Retellable.

Be Relevant

To be *relevant* a story must address itself to the warmth or purpose of the host audience organizations, the complexity or controversy triggered by the topic, the nature of the central problem discussed, or the danger or crisis to be examined. Here's an example:

> You know the wife of a friend of mine recently went along with her husband to attend a sales meeting in Las Vegas. He had won the trip because of his sales leadership. While her husband was tied up in the meetings she slept late. Later wanting to have a good look at the city, she went up to the roof. The warm Nevada sun was so nice that she decided to catch some of it. After a while seeing there was no one around, she took off her two-piece suit and lay down on her stomach and covered her backside with a towel. For some time she lay there until the hotel clerk appeared all agitated and upset.
>
> "Madam, you must come down at once. This is an indecent situation."

"What so you mean?" she said. "There could only be planes above, and anyway I'm covered with a towel."

"Madam," he replied, "don't you realize you are lying over our dining room skylight?"

Well, I'm here to give you another side of the story you might not be aware of.

Franklin Roosevelt told this story in answer to criticism by the press of his administration:

When I was asked whether I read the recent editorials attacking the administration, I remember the advice I learned from Zeke, a mountaineer I encountered in my travels in the South in 1921. Zeke had gone down to visit the doctor about his poor hearing. The doctor examined him and asked how much mountain dew he was drinking a day. Zeke said a quart.

"That's too much," said the doctor. "At that rate you're going to become completely deaf."

Zeke replied, "If it's all the same to you—I'll just become deaf. I like what I've been drinking better than   what I've been hearing."

And, Roosevelt, continued, I understand old Zeke because I don't like some of the things I've been hearing from the Republicans about my bill on the Supreme Court.

A good raconteur like Roosevelt or Reagan knows that he has to tell the story as if it were true. That is why a Johnny Carson or Bob Hope always begins a joke with "Seriously . . . " or "actually. . . . " If a speaker begins a story: "That reminds me of a joke I heard the other day. . . , " such a beginning begs for a flat ending. Do not worry; you cannot be convicted of perjury for telling a fictional anecdote. Just as there is poetic license for authors, there is humor license for speakers.

In the Las Vegas story the speaker tells it as if the incident happened to his neighbor.

Be Realistic

The second rule is that a story should be *realistic*. It does not have to be true but at least it should sound as if it could have happened, and you should tell it as if it did happen.

I simulate a good Churchill, and if I'm invited back to address an audience for the second time, I tell this story:

> In 1931 when Churchill was denouncing his own conservatives as appeasers and the socialists as pacifists he was not the most popular politician. One day the socialist playwright George Bernard Shaw met him on Piccadilly. He said, "Winston, would ye be accepting two tickets to the opening night of my new play. Bring ye a friend if ye have one."
>
> Churchill looked at his calendar and replied, "Unfortunately I cannot attend the opening night. But I would like to attend the second night if there is one!"
> Well, I am happy that you have invited me back for a "second" night.

Never telegraph an audience that you are going to tell a "joke." You have just insured that it will bomb. Second, don't mention the name of the story teller or the source of the anecdote. If you say, "I read this in the *Reader's Digest* the other day and I would like to share . . . ," or "At the convention in Chicago I heard this story about a chicken salesman. . . . ," your joke will fall flat.

To sound *realistic* a story teller must pretend that he is relating straightforwardly an illustrative experience or incident. Much of the laughter is sparked by the unexpected humorous twist. If you telegraph that you are going to tell a joke, you have dissipated the psychological edge for triggering laughter. That is why the same humorous story told in the middle of a speech prompts greater laughter than if it is told at the beginning. Because audiences are not expecting a humorous anecdote at the middle of the talk, they laugh more.

When I am asked how true to the facts a story must be, I recall a negligence case I tried early in my law career. On the stand was a witness to an accident—a trucker in his early thirties.

> I asked, "How far away were you when the accident happened?"
>
> The witness said, "Twenty-two feet, nine and three-quarter inches."
>
> I looked at the court and looked at the jury and said, "Please tell us how you know it was twenty-two feet, nine and three-quarter inches?"
>
> The trucker replied, "When it happened, I took out a tape measure and measured from where I stood to the point of impact, because I knew some jackass of a lawyer was going to ask me that question."

Make Sure It's Retellable

The third rule is that a story must be *retellable*. Will there be people in the audience who would be offended? A speaker should never tell an ethnic joke unless he comes from the same background that is directly or indirectly being made fun of. I have heard a black speaker allude to a watermelon that was served for dessert, and I once witnessed a Jewish businessman tell a story about a Jewish mother. Similarly, if a story is slightly off-color, a test of its appropriateness might be: Could you tell it to your grandmother? Suggestive stories are funny because they skirt the edges of the taboo subject of sex.

For example, rustics may enjoy this story more than city people.

> Jay Wilkinson ran for Congress years ago. Wilkinson, the son of the famous football coach, was an All-American at Duke who married a Miss America finalist after graduating from Harvard Divinity School. Young, handsome, and idealistic, Jay was a perfect subject for Madison Avenue wizardry, which pictured Jay and his wife hand in hand walking through an Oklahoma pasture looking soulfully wistful up at the skies to the accompaniment of soft music with the ad "A Better Tomorrow for all Oklahomans."
>
> The incumbent, Tom Steed, was a good old boy with real sod-kicking credentials. He knew he was in for a tough fight. But he scheduled only a forty-second answer to Wilkinson's spot.
>
> He said to the camera eye, "I may not have a fancy degree from Harvard like young Wilkinson, but I do know enough not to look at the sky when I am walking in a cow pasture." Needless to say, Steed won. And today like Tom Steed I'm not going to be looking up in the sky while I examine this proposal.

To the three Rs of *relevant, realistic,* and *retellable*, I will add the Three Bs, Buildup, Burst, and Bridge. These describe the anatomy of a humorous anecdote tailored to a speech.

Provide a Buildup

A joke demands the *buildup* of tension and then the release of tension to cause the *burst* of laughter. Imagine a balloon. You pump it up with a scenario of details and then you puncture the balloon with the punch line. The polished raconteur does not skimp on the details to rush to the punch line. The following story demands a command of the details.

> I want to say thanks for the last few days. Although I had little to do with the cost and preparation, I had a lot to do with the enjoyment. It recalls the incident of a young man and a blonde who came into a fashionable Fifth Avenue fur store on a Friday afternoon. The man told the clerk in a brusque manner that he wanted to look at the most expensive fur coat in the place. The clerk was doubtful and brought out a nice squirrel-skin job. "Take it away," said the customer. "Apparently you didn't hear what I said. I want the best coat you have."
>
> Next the clerk brought out a beaver coat but again the shopper demurred saying "This isn't your most expensive coat." So finally the clerk shot the works and brought out a $5,000 mutation mink. When the man saw that, his eyes lit up. Turning to the blonde, he said, "That's the idea. Try it on and see how it looks. I want to charge it. Go ahead and check my credit. I'll be back Monday for the coat."
>
> "Certainly, sir, anything you say."
>
> Monday morning the man arrived at the store alone. The minute he walked in, the clerk rushed up to him shaking his fist, followed by the floor walker, the chief buyer, the manager, and the credit manager. All

were shouting at him angrily. "We've looked you up," said the credit manager." You have no more credit than a mouse. You couldn't charge a toothbrush."

"Now calm yourself," said the man. "I haven't taken anything out of your store. I just came in to thank you for   a wonderful *weekend.*

And similarly I'd like to thank everybody. . . .

Incidentally you must *never* write out a joke and then read it. The funniest story will fall flatter and colder than yesterday's pancake if it is read. If you must jot it down, write down the specific details with the punch line in all caps, i.e. "guy—blonde—fur store—1. rabbit 2. beaver 3. mink and finally the punch line—I JUST CAME IN TO THANK YOU FOR A WONDERFUL WEEKEND."

Detonate Laughter with the Trigger Word

The punch line usually features a trigger word that detonates the *burst* of laughter. In this case it is "weekend." The trigger word should be the last word. Often if you put the trigger word before the last, or worse if you forget the trigger word, you step on your own punch line.

Bridging a Joke to Your Theme

You will note that many jokes in the *buildup* use three, i.e., (1) rabbit, (2) beaver, (3) mink. The Rule of Three is often used in the *buildup:* e.g. German, Italian, and Englishman or doctor, lawyer, and priest.

The third B in the three Bs is the *bridge.* The *bridge* is the important link that connects joke to speech, so turning it into humor. The *bridge* is the sentence that makes a humorous story relevant. In the story above, you can use the word "weekend" or say something like "And similarly I'd like to thank everybody . . . " as a bridge to the meat of your speech.

My closing counsel reminds me of the warning a biology professor of mine gave a young coed. This particularly beautiful student was stunned when the biology professor asked her, "What part of the human body enlarges to about ten times its normal measurement during periods of emotion or excitement?" "I . . . I refuse to answer that question," the girl stammered as she shyly avoided looking at her male classmates sitting nearby. One of them was called upon next, and he correctly answered, "The pupil of the eye."

"Miss Rogers," said the professor, "your refusal to answer my question makes three things evident. First, you didn't study last night's assignment. Second, you have a dirty mind. And third," concluded the professor, "I'm afraid marriage is going to be a tremendous disappointment for you."

And similarly the speaker who has bought my book and then says he still feels awkward about telling a story makes three things clear. First, he hasn't read the book through and sampled the variety of anecdotes available. Second, he has a dull mind if he isn't able to build one of these stories into his speech topic. And third, speaking, instead of being a lot of fun, will be a chore and a disappointment.

Chapter 15

Some Tips for Women

Nancy Astor in her youth was a beauty who moved to England, married a peer, and became the first women to be elected to the House of Commons. (Her twin sister, by the way, was the model who inspired the Gibson girl.)

On one occasion some men tried to taunt Nancy Astor as the fashionable lady member of Parliament was propounding some of her proposals on women's rights.

A heckler in the back, referring to the necklace and many bracelets the bejeweled Lady Astor wore, jibed, "You have enough brass on you, Lady Astor, to make a kettle."

"And," replied Lady Astor, "you have enough water in your head to fill it."

Unfortunately a lot of men do have water on their brain—at least in their perception of women speakers. They have advanced little from Samuel Johnson's eighteenth century opinion of a woman delivering a sermon. "Sir, a woman's preaching is like a dog's walking on its hinder legs. It is not done well; but you are surprised to

Some Tips for Women

find it done at all." These chauvinist types, while they grant that some women like Margaret Thatcher, Jean Kirkpatrick, or Barbara Jordan can hold an audience's attention, think that the typical woman is too emotional and flighty to deliver a reasonable appeal or, at the very least, the pitch of her voice too strident and the pace of her delivery too rapid to inspire an audience.

Forget for a moment that Abraham Lincoln had a high-pitched voice or that Hubert Humphrey spoke in a machine-gun delivery. Women must be prepared to battle such prejudices. Women, like Avis, must try harder.

In the 1930s and the 1940s one of the most popular afternoon radio soap operas was *Portia Faces Life*, the continuing story of a woman making her way as a careerist in a man's world. Of course, the title took its name from Shakespeare's heroine in *Merchant of Venice*, who disguises herself as a male lawyer in the successful effort to save Antonio whose life could be taken for his forfeited pledge to Shylock for "a pound of flesh."

The amazed Shylock wonders at "his" advocacy and says, "I never knew so young a boy with so old a head."

In fact, as Portia proved, youth and fair looks are never liabilities in a speaker's appearance unless it is not combined with brains. On the other hand, a woman does not have to be beautiful to be a commanding speaker. Jean Kirkpatrick and Barbara Jordan prove that. In fact, height and bulk, if sometimes deemed less desirable attributes of a woman, are an asset to the woman speaker. It enhances her authority, but it is no more essential than possessing a low voice.

129

Slow Down Your Pace

Still a modern Portia must face the facts of life. It is true that the lower-pitched and slower-paced voice is easier on the ears and is easier to understand—a fact well known to radio, television, and advertising executives—and women do tend to speak higher and faster. A high pitch is often a sign of excitement. All voices tend to rise when their owners are aroused by conviction or anger. The easiest way to keep a voice from soaring to the upper ranges is to apply the brakes. If you slow up your pace, you will tone down the voice.

Before my voice changed, my two older brothers would tease me about my "girlish" voice. The angrier I got, the faster and higher I spoke—and the more my brothers laughed. Eventually my voice changed, but my rapid pace of speaking did not. Some years later a psychologist who was a copanelist with me at a speech workshop told me that rapid speaking may be a sign of insecurity. The talker wants to get everything in before the audience walks away. In my case, he suggested that perhaps by speaking fast I was trying to get in my say before my brothers' attention wandered.

At any rate, I have learned to slow down my delivery. The easiest place to practice is on the telephone. Take a deep breath before you speak. A slower voice will be a deeper voice. One woman I know who has deliberately worked on her telephone voice says she has scraps of paper in her desk drawer corresponding to IOUs in drinks from men who have never met her personally but know her only from her telephone voice. They all have eagerly promised to take her out for a drink if and when they get to her city.

A TV actress once told me that she learned to speak more slowly just by taking lessons in diction. At a voice school she was taught to enunciate more clearly by punctuating the ends of participles—sounding the *g*'s. As a result, the more careful way of speaking slowed her pace and even lowered her tonal register, thus winning her assignments she formerly would have lost.

Deeper breaths and clearer diction take practice, and practice is the only way one can overcome the root cause of an overly high-strung nervousness.

Speak to the Point: Know Your Facts

Poise is a matter of experience. When you do speak at a staff meeting, obey the first rule: Do not rise to speak in a staff session or a board meeting unless you have facts to reinforce your opinion. Male executives may use such discussions to vent their pet peeves about private worries. While this is not an effective technique for them, it is disastrous for women. Men may meander along without coming to a point and not run a serious risk to their professional esteem. Women do so at their peril.

I know a woman in a national toy concern who bragged to me of her intuition in picking what games would catch on with the preteen set. But when I asked her whether she gave public credit to her intuition at the sales conference meetings, she replied:

"Hell, no. You think I'm crazy? My predecessor was also a woman. She used to be laughed at behind her back for always quoting the opinions of her favorite niece—even though, as far as I could tell, that niece of hers had better instincts than some who make the buying decisions.

"I have my sources, too, Jamie, but I never reveal them. I disguise all hunches with a few calls to some selected stores. Then I look at all the sales surveys for data that

131

back up my opinion. I even clip articles from magazines or newspapers that might lend added weight.

"After five years of doing this, I now get respect when I stand up. A couple of days before any meeting, I look for the weakest link in last month's sales—chance games, puzzles, physical skill challenges—and zero in on it. Usually I have a hunch or an educated guess, and I call some of my friends in department stores to see if I can't translate these hunches into statistics."

Avoid Gossip

A colleague of mine in the State Department in Washington was not so incisive in her comments at staff meetings, and her rate of promotion suffered because of it. She had the habit of interspersing her comments on her bureau's activities for the past month with all kinds of asides about the various personalities she had to deal with. She developed the reputation of being overly chatty and gossipy.

It is true that some of the men in the same report session laced their reports with heavy humor about their respective golf games or recent bets in the pro football pool, but such banter did not come off as frivolous—at least not to the predominantly male members at the conference table. The men's reports weren't, on the average, shorter than hers. It just seemed that way to the men. So rule Number 2: Don't be chatty or gossipy.

Men can often be myopic in their assessments. A recent survey reveals that men believed they strode briskly on city streets but that women strolled leisurely—looking at shop windows. Actually, the reverse was true—at least during the lunch hour. Women are racing purposefully to get a few errands done in that allotted amount of time. Men are more apt to take casual saunters, alternating between being sidewalk shoppers and girl watchers.

The same is true about talking. In Congress it is not the women who have among their membership the windiest talkers. The length of speeches in *The Congressional Record* proves that the female members are briefer in their reported remarks.

Be Assertive

One of the reasons that women tend to deliver shorter talks, particularly to mixed audiences, is that many of them find that standing and speaking to a seated audience is an unnerving experience. Basically, it's an authoritarian role, and women are conditioned from birth against assuming such a commanding air.

Because many women are uncomfortable in take-charge situations, they often tend to speak in tentative tones—phrasing as questions what should be stated assertively. A brilliant insurance executive in Hartford was a wizard at financial planning. Yet she was passed over for a vice presidency because she sounded like a high schooler the first time she was called on to give a report at a board meeting.

To associates in her firm she would preface her comments on possible investments with something like, "I know the real estate market with the mortgage rate so high may not seem so good at first, but isn't it possible that. . . . " Or she would say, "Perhaps I'm being too speculative on this. . . . " But the problem was more than her words—it was the hesitation in her voice, the delays in her delivery, the waiting for nods of reassurance. She was liked by her superiors, but popularity did not spell the right promotion. Brasher but less capable men advanced over her. All because she was too tentative and did not assert her expertise in firm declarative sentences.

Practice, Practice, Practice

A woman journalist who is a popular speaker once confessed to me that she had enrolled in a Dale Carnegie course when she was in her first job out of college. "It was sort of like Weight Watchers. I didn't feel self-conscious in front of a lot of fatties. Neither did I mind speaking in front of other timid souls—people I didn't know or have anything in common with. What I got out of it was the wonderful practice of getting up and speaking to an audience."

If the thought of that is too embarrassing, then look up the nearest toastmaster's club. In one year you will get more opportunities to speak than you will in the next ten years of business life. Practice may not make you perfect, but it will reduce the fear that you have to be perfect. The more times you speak outside your job, the easier you'll find standing on your feet and addressing an audience.

Don't refuse any opportunity to speak or appear on a panel. You should not only accept speaking invitations, but seek them. If the fear even after frequent talks doesn't disappear, take the advice of Gloria Steinem. "Do it anyway, sister, and pray *She* will help you!"

Chapter 16

Dealing with Hostile Questions

At a ship christening in Glasgow, the head of the British Woman's Temperance Union accosted Winston Churchill, the First Lord of the Admiralty. "Minister," she cried, "we think it is a horrid example for British youth to launch ships with champagne."

"On the contrary, Madam Chairman," Churchill retorted, "it is a splendid example of temperance. The ship takes its first sip of wine and then proceeds on water ever after."

We read of Churchill's retorts to Lady Astor, Bessie Braddock, George Bernard Shaw, and others, and yearn to have his knack for the snappy comeback that squelches the heckler.

For most of us, a hostile question triggers an immediate, angry answer that is fueled in the blaze of passions. The speaker who responds in kind to the unfriendly questioner does not usually come off well to his audience. He tries to swing from his heels for a home run, but all he does manage to hit is air—hot air. It is better not to emulate Babe Ruth but Pete Rose. Don't aim at the fences for that perfect squelch. Just try to meet the curve ball and hit it safely.

Remember the perfect comeback is never devised in the heat of passion. You think of it in the cool reflection later on. It is what the French writer Diderot called staircase wit *(l'esprit d'escalier)*, the reply you think of when you climb the stairs to bed after the living room argument.

A speaker, when he descends from the authority of a featured speaker to mix it up with a hostile questioner, loses some of his prestige and increases that of his challenger. When his reply is impulsive, he's pitting emotion against emotion. The less cool his reply, the less command he has of the audience. When he yields this advantage, he is playing on the turf of his questioner.

If Possible, Prepare for Hostile Questions

The most foolproof insurance against making a fool of yourself is to prepare answers to hostile questions the night before you give the speech. As a speech writer in the White House, I often had the task of devising hypothetical questions and framing answers to them before a scheduled Presidential press conference. Answers of two or three sentences can be worked out to respond to the trickiest questions in the cool abstraction of the desk or study. You don't even have to memorize your written answers. Just the process of writing them out should be enough.

Hostile question: "When are your utilities going to stop gouging the consumers by raising the price of electricity?"

Answer: "The price of electricity, like that of bread,

butter, and everything else in our free market, is governed by the law of supply and demand. Power is like any other commodity—if there is a demand for it, the price goes up. To bring the prices down is like running water uphill."

Let's say you have given a speech as a utilities executive many times. You would not be surprised by the appearance of hostile questions. You would have contacted the public affairs office and asked for a fact summary or a question-and-answer sheet.

But if your company does not have a public relations department, you're going to have to devise some answers yourself. Sometimes you get word that someone is lying in wait for you.

A friend of mine who is on the board of a private school heard that a faculty member was going to attack her about a recent decision of the trustees to build a private residence for the new headmistress.

The woman called me and asked if I would frame a good answer to the angry questioner.

I helped her to devise a ready answer, but I suggested that the primary strategy in such a case was to defuse the question in the course of her talk.

> I share the concern of all the faculty people that salaries are too low. That is why I can understand why some of your question our pledge to build a house on campus for the new headmistress. When the new headmistress was selected—by the enthusiastic recommendation of faculty representatives—we made such a pledge. But that does not weaken our commitment to seek more endowment and higher salaries for the rest of the faculty; on the contrary, it reinforces it. . . . We are now all the more committed to seek higher salaries."

137

Because of that paragraph in her speech to the faculty, a nasty confrontation never developed.

Delay and Depersonalize Your Response by Repeating the Question

Sometimes there is no advance warning about hostile questions. In such situations the first rule is to insulate yourself from the impact of the question.

A bank vice president whom I heard speak in a neighborhood forum began the process of insulating himself when he took his version of a "beating your wife" question.

"When are you going to stop jacking up the mortgage rates so high that poor people can't buy houses?"

He listened intently to the hostile questioner and then wheeled to the other side of the audience and repeated the question, adding, "The question concerns the establishment of mortgage rates."

The process of repeating the question is seen as a courteous gesture to make sure the entire audience understands the question, but it serves to cool off the hot, aggressive tone of the question. An immediate answer would have produced the direct and personal confrontation of a two-man argument. The potentially nasty situation was depersonalized into an opportunity for group discussion. By repeating the question, he gave himself time to think of an effective answer.

> When farmers raise the price of butter, the supermarkets that buy that butter also have to increase their prices. Similarly, banks get their money from the government. When the Federal Reserve Board raises its discount rate, we have to increase the cost of borrow-

138

ing to the consumer because our cost of borrowing is higher.

Don't Continue with the Same Questioner

Although the audience was generally satisfied by his answer, the hostile questioner tried to engage him in another question. The banker, however, cut him off by recognizing another questioner.

He refused to be drawn into a two-man shouting match, which would only degrade his stature and demean his authority. He wisely chose to answer someone else. This is exactly what the President does in a press conference. He tries to avoid follow-up questions. The rest of the audience is supportive because they tend to resent those who try to hog the question period.

If Possible, Break Down the Question into Two Parts

In the situation with the banker, it turned out that the next questioner was just as hostile.

"When are the banks going to stop picking up the discounted commercial paper of those fly-by-night operations that cheat poor people when they sell them shoddy appliances?"

Again the banker depersonalized the question by repeating it to another part of the room, but he also "dissected" the question.

> The question about installment-plan purchases of refrigerators and other home appliances is really two questions.

First, should you prevent those stores from selling washing machines or television sets on credit to people who are so hard up that they couldn't get a loan to buy those appliances at a bank? The answer is even if you wanted to, you couldn't. It is not possible to stop people from buying what they want—even if they don't have the means. It would be like stopping them from spending their paychecks on liquor or gambling. So they but refrigerators or TVs on notes.

The second question involves the bank notes. These notes are a form of money. We can no more check on the individual history of all of those notes than you can have a detective track down the history of each fifty-dollar bill you receive. If we tried to, the whole banking system would shut down. So the answer is not in reforming the banks but in reforming the consumer laws and educating the public.

Almost any hostile question can be broken down into two parts. This is to the responder's advantage: Not only does it help him organize his answer better, but he can use the division as double insulation against the anger or hostility in the question.

Handling Assumptive Questions

On Sunday panel shows like *Meet the Press* or *Face the Nation*, where a politician or a diplomat confronts the questions of veteran reporters, one often sees another variation of the dissection technique. This consists of extracting the "assumption" from the hostile question.

"Dr. Robertson, do you think your opposition to Jews or anyone who does not share your Christian values is good politics for winning Republican Presidential primaries?"

> The question carries the assumptions that I am anti-Israel, when just the opposite is true. I have visited Israel many times, and I believe leaders there would tell you that no one has been a stronger supporter of Israel or a more staunch defender of its security. It is true that I, as a Christian, support Christian values, but that does not mean I oppose Jewish values. Indeed, Jewish values are an integral part of our Judeo-Christian ethic.

Although the political leader is expected to field almost any kind of question tossed to him, the speaker in the ordinary situation can set his own ground rules. If after the end of the speech he asks that questions be limited to his area of knowledge, he will actually focus and intensify his reputation as an expert.

Don't Hesitate to Say, "I Don't Know"

Finally, there is nothing more refreshing than the speaker who simply replies, "I don't know the answer to that."

A consultant to the Republican National Committee recently was advising young candidates for Congress on campaign techniques.

"Let me give you one magic phrase to use in response if you are asked a question about which you know little or nothing—and you're going to be asked a lot of these questions: 'I don't know, but I sure as heck intend to find out.' "

In this age of political cynicism, the candidate who admits to his ignorance about what he doesn't know gains much more credibility on what he does know. The final comment of the campaign consultant was, "The innocent is going to win a lot more votes than the smart aleck."

Don't Try to Be a Smart Aleck

Sometimes a speaker who is personally attacked snaps back with a cute rejoinder. Few can be witty on the spur of the moment. Don't try it!

It is better to say, as Henry Ford II once did to a group of consumers advocates, "I will answer all fair questions, but not loaded ones."

I once found myself confronted in a question period by someone who launched into a lengthy diatribe against the organization I represented.

I answered, "I am obliged to answer questions, but not harangues masquerading as questions."

Such replies, given in a cool, matter-of-fact tone, are better than trying to come up with the cute retort. Fred Allen once said of Jack Benny, who relied on a team of gag writers, "Jack couldn't ad-lib a belch after a Hungarian dinner."

The clever put-down to a hostile question tends to beof a personal nature. If it is not very clever, the would-be squelcher suffers more than his antagonist, for he has more to lose. To repeat, the speaker will lose in the confrontation, for he will have dragged himself down to the level of the questioner.

To recapitulate, the best strategy in answering a hostile question is to *delay, depersonalize, dissect,* and *deflect.*

Delay the impact of the nasty query by repeating it, not to the questioner, but to another part of the audience.

Depersonalize the question by rephrasing it in a more neutral way.

Dissect the question either by breaking it into parts or by extracting the unfair assumption.

Deflect the question by giving a response to your re-phrasing of it. Your answer does not have to be an exact response to the person's query as long as it is a true answer to your interpretation of the question.

To deflect a curve ball question is to watch for the spin on the ball and manage to make contact and hit safely. If you do that, you are not going to hit a home run but will get a high average for base hits. Remember Babe Ruth held for many years the record for strikeouts as well as home runs. On the other hand, Pete Rose, king of the single, will win entry into the Hall of Fame for his concentration on meeting every pitch, instead of trying to slug it out of the park.

Chapter 17

How to Make Visual Aids a Prop, Not a Crutch

Some years ago I was asked as a communications consultant to speak to a conference of a major oil company at a corporate retreat in Tennessee. Before I addressed the group at 3:30 P.M., a representative of a psychological testing company specializing in corporate management spoke to the 200 assembled. He had the lights turned out and then paraded a series of complicated graphs, which purportedly showed the flow of decision-making in the corporate world. After about forty minutes, I heard a peculiar buzz that I thought was due to a faulty machine projecting the slides. Actually it was the snores produced by the combination of both the torpor of after-lunch digestion and the tedium of a slide presentation.

"The Tongue Can Paint What the Eye Can't See"

We all have heard the Chinese maxim, "One picture is worth a thousand words." Less familiar is another saying, "The tongue can paint what the eye can't see." If that seems a contradiction, consider this: the more successful presentations use visual aids, but so do the most boring.

It all depends on whether the speaker uses his slides or exhibits as a prop or as a crutch. Are the visual aids the seasoning that bring out the flavor or are they the meal itself?

Several years ago, at a meeting held at the Union Club in New York City, I heard a talk on World War I. The speaker had written a fascinating book based on oral reminiscences of veterans. Since I was to introduce him, I had not only read the book but made a point of engaging him in conversation at the head table. He proved to converse as interestingly as he wrote.

Yet, the speech that followed was not a talk, but a series of introductions to slides. "And here is a picture of the tank used at the Battle of the Somme. . . . And here is a picture of General Pershing." In the book, the description of the Battle of the Somme and the characterization of Black Jack Pershing were far more vivid and memorable than the one-dimensional photographs. The speaker had subordinated himself to the slide projector, and his speech was little more than verbal captions for a disjointed series of pictures.

The problem is that it is easier to think of some introductory comments to each slide than to prepare a proper presentation with slides used as dramatic emphasis. Visual displays should not be a security blanket to hide behind, but rather a handkerchief to pull out of the sleeve. Otherwise, the speaker comes off second-best and the slides are shown to their worst advantage.

A travel agent I know was trying to promote a Bermuda package tour to an association. When she looked in her briefcase, she found she had forgotten the photographs of the beach and hotel. Nevertheless, she didn't cancel her appointment, but worked up notes in her room from what she remembered when she had stayed in Bermuda a few years before. To the association director she waxed poetic about an old pirate cove where couples could rent a boat and drift in the glow of an island sunset. She painted a picture of romantic bike rides with picnic lunches prepared by the hotel. She exulted about the perfect blend of island charm and quaint old English village. Well, she won her sale even though no one from her agency had ever managed to sell that association a package travel deal before.

She later told me, "It was a great step in my career development—not that I didn't need the picture packet, but I learned the real secret to selling."

Sell Yourself First

Top salesmen—be they insurance agents from the million-dollar round table or door-to-door brush peddlers—will tell you that if you sell yourself first, the product almost sells itself.

But when the speaker or salesman shifts the major burden of persuasion to slides or samples, he will make no lasting impression on his audience. He comes off not as a dynamic authority, but as a drab assistant who runs the projector and flips through the exhibits.

Yet why do so many top corporate executives make the mistake of demeaning themselves by deferring to their visual aids? Well, one could say that Americans—particularly in the business world—have a naive faith in anything mechanical. They are suckers for any new gadget or contraption that they think will do their work for them. But there is a more basic reason: fear. The fear of getting up before an audience to speak. Oh, they don't admit it. Ranking executives instead will say to me when I visit them as a communications consultant, "Look, I'm not on any ego trip. I don't care if I don't come off as a big shot. I just want to get the facts across, and the best way to do that is with these slides and graphs." And then they unfailingly add, "You know a picture is proof." And my answer to them is that a series of pictures is no substitute for the personal beliefs and experiences of the speaker.

Visual Aids as Reinforcement, Not Competition

Visual aids should be used to reinforce the speech, not replace it. The aid should not deflect attention from the actor, nor should it detract from the message. One corporate head of a utilities conglomerate effectively used a chart comparing tonnage on trucking, rail, and shipping lines, but he did it this way. He had the chart posted at the rear of the audience room. Then, toward the end of his speech, he strode off the podium to the back of the room. People turned expectantly around, fixing their eyes on the clearly marked chart even before the speaker reached it. Though the red, green, blue, and black colors marking the comparative traffic totals were self-explanatory, the speaker exploited the audience's focusing on the chart as a good way to encapsulate and end his talk.

One of the worst presentations I ever saw was staged by an executive who should have known better. The president of one of the nation's top advertising and public relations agencies used a series of slides as the basis of his talk, but during much of the time he had a large television console running video tapes of some of his agencies' advertisements.

147

The result was a three-ring circus where the two other side shows diverted attention away from the central performer.

It you use visual aids, project one at a time. When you move to another topic, the slide should be removed or replaced with a blank black one so that the audience's attention is not diverted.

Keep Them Simple

Your visual aids should also not be so complex that they defy an easy grasp or understanding. In fact, the most effective ones, at times, are those you can construct yourself in the midst of your presentation. I once witnessed the president of an oil company achieve this effect in front of an audience. He had put building blocks—the kind kids play with—behind him on the speaker's table, to make his point that profits in the movie and chemical industries had jumped to much higher levels than those in the oil company. He piled up different-colored blocks, uttering statistics as he did so. The dramatic use of the blocks registered to the eye, and thereby to the mind, how relatively little were the gains for the oil industry. The contrasting pile of blocks was more arresting than any complex graph with various lines zigzagging and crisscrossing up and down.

A friend of mine is a vice president of one of the leading national companies that creates corporate identities through logos. To sell the idea, he carries with him a flannel board that can be propped up on the table or hung on a wall. As he talks, he slaps on familiar and recognizable logos in a decal size. The manual action enlivens the presentation by directing the eyes of the audience to each different logo. If, instead, there had been a board behind him with all the various logos, the audience would have been distracted and their listening attention diverted.

Now, the reader might ask if my friend was not "introducing" each decal or logo and thus violating the advice I gave earlier. The answer is no, because the exhibit was so simple that it needed no explanation. The rule is that if you have to spend a lot of time explaining the slide or exhibit, you shouldn't use it in your talk. Instead prepare a brochure or pamphlet that includes explanatory notes, and pass out the item at the end of your talk or presentation.

Most visual aids, unless simple and used sparingly, will kill a speech and deaden the attention of the audience. Remember, not all graphs are graphic nor all posters imposing. Think of a visual aid like a magazine-page advertisement—if the picture is not self-explanatory and can't be summed up quickly in a simple, catchy tag line, don't trot it out.

A visual display should not be a security blanket to hide behind, but rather a handkerchief to pull out of your sleeve. To keep a prop from becoming a crutch, I offer the Ten Commandments of Visual Aids.

> I. Thou shalt not use displays which are not bold, simple, and arresting in appeal. Cluttered or busy displays blur the message and bore the audience.
>
> II. Thou shalt not have the captions on the exhibits with more than three or four lines of written text. Ideally the caption should be as short as that of a billboard poster.
>
> III. Thou shalt not overburden the display with

"corporatese" or technical jargon. Try to use the language of the advertising copywriter—simple, short, and clear.

IV. Thou shalt not make the printer text so small that it cannot be seen clearly from the back of the room.

V. Thou shalt not keep the pointer or directing stick in your hand throughout the speech. Nothing is more distracting than a waving stick. A pointer is not a pacifier for the edgy speaker; it is an arrow. Put the pointer down when you are through pointing.

VI. Thou shalt not make the whole presentation in a darkened room. You might find some of the audience falling asleep, particularly after a heavy meal.

VII. Thou shalt not leave an exhibit in view when you have finished discussing it. Unless you are comparing various samples, models, or displays, remove a previous exhibit. It is helpful to use a black slide to cover up the previous frame.

VIII. Thou shalt not use linear graphs which zigzag across the screen. Instead use the vertical bars of different colors to show comparisons in costs and profits.

IX. Thou shalt not read your speech off the slides. Medical doctors are the worst violators of this rule. Their notes are printed right on the slides underneath their visuals. The audience can read too!

X. Thou shalt not deliver a commentary on a series of exhibits or slides. A presentation should not be a parade of exhibits, nor a speech a series of slides with verbal asides or marginal remarks sandwiched in between.

A speaker is not an engineer, but an executive. In fact, he is a *leader* at least for the time he presides over the podium for that audience. Yet he denotes himself to mere technician when he takes a backseat to the slides. When the slides become a crutch, he is professionally a cripple—a lame excuse for an executive. But if he uses his visual aids as props, he elevates not only himself but the audience's understanding of his message.

Chapter 18

Some Extra Steps to Spark Audience Response

Adlai Stevenson, "I'm here to speak, and you're here to listen, and if you finish before me, feel free to leave." Stevenson knew that the audience also has a role in shaping a good presentation. The speaker is not the sole determinant, and the good speaker tries to make sure that the audience will be working with him and not against him.

To do that the speaker must create some enthusiasm (or at least interest) in his upcoming talk.

Picking the Right Title

Well, the first priority in insuring a strong turnout for your talk is to pick the right *title*. Titles such as "Perspectives of the Life Insurance Industry" will discourage attendance, yet a title for the same talk could be "You Could Live to Ninety."

The more imaginative the title, the easier it is for the program chairman to promote interest in your talk. After all, you presumably don't have a household name that will draw a crowd on its own strength. If you are a business consultant speaking on the cash-flow problem, call it "Cash Flow—Turning a Trickle into a Torrent." A home builder might entitle a talk "A Contractor Looks at Tomorrow's Building Costs." I once heard an investment analyst speak on "Tapping the Money Well."

A talk I delivered often in 1987, the bicentennial year of the Constitutional Convention, is entitled "What's Happening at the Convention, Dr. Franklin?" Another talk popular with women's groups is my speech on the First Ladies. I call it "Pink Ladies, Blue Stockings, and Green Hornets: The Inside Secrets of our Nation's First Ladies." A lecture I deliver to medical groups on authors who once practiced as physicians is entitled "My Son, the Doctor, I Mean the Author."

A would-be author called on Somerset Maugham one afternoon to ask his advice for picking a title for the novel he had just completed.

"Mr. Maugham, I've just written a novel but have been unable to come up with an intriguing title. Your books have such wonderful titles—*Cakes and Ale, The Razor's Edge, Moon and Sixpence*. Could you help me with my title by reading the book?"

"There is no necessity for reading your book," replied Maugham. "Are there drums in it?"

"No, it's not that kind of story. You see, it deals . . ."

"Are there any bugles in it?"

"No, certainly not" was the response.

"Well then," replied the famous author, "call it *No Drums, No Bugles*."

Somerset Maugham knew that the title of a book is its packaging. The same is true with a speech.

A title is the packaging of a talk. Bright packaging creates anticipation and expectation. It also suggests that the speaker will be as interesting and entertaining as the title.

Know Your Audience

The next *T* to cross in getting the audience to work for you is to know the *type* of audience you are addressing. Is it mostly senior citizens you are addressing? Is it strictly a businessman audience or are the businessmen bringing their wives?

Don't rely completely on the title of the organization.

When I was in the State Department, I was scheduled to talk to a chapter of university women in suburban Chicago. In my mind's eye I pictured them as equivalent to the League of Women Voters. When I arrived, I found that in outlook and manner they were closer to the DAR! By observing their clothes and listening to their conversation, I sensed that the women were conservative and traditional. I changed my speech accordingly.

Another time I was invited to address a Savings and Loan League in New Jersey. I expected a group of bankers, but to my surprise I found that most of the audience was made up of young girls in their twenties with beehive hairdos who were being treated by their bosses to a night out in a special festive banquet. Surprises like these force one to reshape the tone of one's remarks.

Now in both cases, if I had taken the time to call the program chairman beforehand, I might not have been surprised by the audience.

I find people are not offended if you say, "Is the estimated median age about forty to fifty?" Or "Do you expect the audience to be about half and half men and women?" To find out the cultural or educational background, you might ask who were the most popular speakers recently and why?

One way to prevent surprises is to *intermingle* before the speech. Attend the reception before the dinner (but restrict your libations to cola or juice).

Check Out the Program

At those receptions the program chairman usually introduces to you a few people. Make it a point to ask him who else is to speak and what presentations or awards (if any) are going to be made. First, it may be possible for you to include the mention of an awardee as an example of dedication, voluntary action, or civic service. Look up at the head table when you are attending a banquet and note that the speaker is often scribbling on his program. Usually he is trying to work in some of the head table dignitaries and awardees to his talk. Secondly, if others are to speak, you may have to curtail the length of your talk. It makes a difference if you are the only speaker or one of several in the program. Failure to check out the format of the program can be fatal.

I recall an occasion when, because of a late place connection, I arrived at a Madison, Wisconsin, service club for a talk on Churchill halfway through the lunch. During the talk, I said how Churchill possessed this Dickensian faculty for seeing nouns in surnames. "Remember," I said, "how Churchill made the name of 'Quisling' a new synonym for traitor." My talk, which prompted no applause, was followed by an award to a doctor who had served the community of Madison for many years—Dr. Norge Quisling!

If Possible, Mingle with Your Listeners— Before You Speak

At these receptions, I always anticipate meeting at least one in the audience who knows me or one of my family. This has included former classmates from grade school to law school as well as former associates who once worked professionally with me in government or business. I have spoken in every state but Alaska, and it seems that in almost every talk, I have found a mutual friend.

For that reason I always make it a rule to visit with as many people as possible at any reception before the talk. Even if I do not meet up with any old friends or acquaintances, I establish some mutual bond in finding out where they hail from, what college they attended, or what they do. Later, from the vantage point of the head table, I search them out and find their place in the audience. During my talk I will try to fix my eyes upon them even if only for a moment. Invariably they are the ones who start a ripple of laughter or trigger a burst of applause.

The reason nightclub comedians hate to work to small crowds is because they know that they have to work harder for laughs. It only takes one uninhibited listener to trigger a burst of laughter from his fellow listeners. The bigger the crowd, the greater likelihood there is of having several or even a host of these uproarious types whose laughter is contagious.

Opera singers used to hire claques to make sure that rounds of applause were initiated. They knew that one person could ignite a whole music hall into a standing ovation.

I don't recommend organizing a claque unless you are a political candidate, but I do say that every connection you establish with a member of the audience before your talk increases the chances of a hearty reception.

But the most important reason for circulating among the group who will soon be listening to you is to get a feel of the audience.

Of course, the most important person to talk to is the program chairman or whoever is to introduce you.

Supplying Your Biography for Your "Introduction"

It is essential to ask him roughly what he will mention about your background. Biographical details such as a book or article published or certain experience in a volunteer agency might be crucial in laying down the foundation for expertise in the particular talk you are giving.

Usually I send the program chairman a sample *introduction*. That is because my pet hate is the introduction that seems to be read verbatim from my résumé without any effort to organize it into a graceful introduction. The audience wants a prologue, not a catalog of biographical entries and statistics.

To prevent that, I often, in my correspondence to the program chairman, include photostats of two introductions used on previous occasions. Actually I have written these myself in a witty brief format that makes me as well as the introducer look good.

> Our speaker as you can see is a large man and the scope
> of his activities and accomplishments is just as large.

157

> He is, or has been, a lawyer, legislator, actor, diplomat,
> professor, author, business consultant, and speech writer
> to three Presidents. But whether he is arguing in court,
> debating in assembly, lecturing in class, authoring ten
> books, or writing speeches for three Presidents, two
> interests seem to dominate—the love of history and
> the English language. That is why it comes as no sur-
> prise that a hero of our speaker is Winston Churchill,
> whom he met while an exchange student in England in
> 1953. Mr. Humes, who is a friend of the Churchill fam-
> ily, authored a prize-winning biography, *Churchill,
> Speaker of the Century*. Ladies and Gentlemen, James
> Humes, "An Evening with Churchill."

Of course there is no guarantee that the program chairman will use it, but at least it encourages him to frame the
introduction in a graceful narrative fashion.

Of course even if you have seen a copy of the introduction, it is no guarantee that things will go smoothly. At the
University of Fudan in Shanghai, I was to deliver a lecture
entitled "Richard Nixon: From Chiang Kai-Shek Advocate
to Chou En-lai Admirer." I had forwarded an advance copy
of my speech to them, and they, in turn, had sent me their
draft of a rather long and fulsome introduction. At the head
table one of my hosts rose and delivered a ten-minute talk
in Chinese. It was followed by restrained applause in which
I heartily joined until an embassy aide nudged me. "I
wouldn't do that, Mr. Humes. You are applauding your own
introduction."

In sending your introduction or résumé, be sure to include a glossy picture of yourself. Even if the newspapers
do not publish it, they are more likely to run a story if you
do a professional job; include a press kit that contains a
release, a photograph, and a biographical résumé with your

telephone number for additional inquiries. The release, which they can run with minimal editing, should mention you, the title of your talk, the date and place of your appearance, the name of the host organization, and a brief account of what you are going to say.

If the newspaper runs the story announcing in advance your appearance, you will get the word to professional and personal acquaintances who might not know that you will be making a talk. People who do business with your firm might also make it a point to attend or get invited by a friend or associate to hear you. Those friends or mutual acquaintances always seem to seek you out at the reception and become your enthusiastic listeners and applauders.

Investigate the Banquet Room or Meeting Hall

Even more important than seeing the program chairman is *investigating* the banquet room or meeting hall. Try out the public address system. I for example prefer a lavaliere mike—the kind that comes fixed on the lapel—because I like to move around and not be tied to the stationary microphone. Although I ask for it in advance, sometimes I find it has not been made available. If one can't be located, I work with what is given me, but I always check it out.

Once I was to be introduced by Olivia de Havilland, the renowned actress. Even though she was not bearing the main brunt of the speaking, she went to the banquet room early and checked on the mike. She stationed me in the very back of the room and then spoke softly to make sure her voice could be heard.

On one occasion in Vancouver, British Columbia, I found myself in the center of a wide, shallow rectangular room. To look at the audience I constantly had to make a turn of my head in a hard right or left. The problem was that, when I turned that way, the microphone did not pick up my voice. Check the range of the microphone and how sensitive it is in receiving the voice.

If the public address system fails in the middle of your talk, don't panic; it happens all the time. Say something like—"Mr. Nixon is not the only one who has problems with microphones" and wait until they fix it.

If you are speaking in an assembly hall or auditorium rather than in a banquet hall, ask the program chairman to insist that attendees fill up the front of an empty hall. Nothing kills the effect of a speaker more than acres of dead space between you and the front row of listeners. Once, after I had addressed the Pennsylvania Bar Association, a program chairman said, "Humes, you were great but not as great as you were when you spoke to the Philadelphia Bar Association." I replied, "It was the same speech. The only difference is you had twenty yards of empty space before me that was to be used for the dancers after I talked. That dead space made the difference."

Closing Remarks

Many speakers end their talk by formally expressing their appreciation for the opportunity to address them. Such anticlimactic statements invite only polite applause.

If you must show your gratitude to the host organization, do it in the middle of the talk, when praise is more sincerely believed.

But when you have finished your speech, don't utter but

whisper your *thanks*. Mouth your "thank you" with a slight acknowledging nod.

Crossing the *t*'s and dotting the *i*'s by choosing a snappy *title*, providing a good *introduction*, *intermingling* with your audience, and *investigating* the podium won't make a poor talk good, but faulty or sloppy arrangements can make a fine address come off mediocre.

Chapter 19

Lawyer, Teacher or Preacher: Three Kinds of Speaker

In just about every speech we are either advocating a cause, explaining a concept, or commemorating an occasion. Those different approaches suggest different formulas:

When a speaker is exhorting or persuading, he is an Advocate. As a lawyer talks to the jury, so the Advocate speaker is persuading an audience to adopt his view. Similarly a speaker is an Advocate when he tries to sell a program, urge a policy, or rally a nation.

On the other hand, when a speaker is recounting an experience or explaining a discovery, he is more like a Teacher or Professor. He is a Lecturer making the complex understandable and the exotic familiar.

The third kind of speech is the "dedication or commemorative talk." Here the speaker is more like a Preacher. He doesn't exhort like the lawyer or explain like the teacher. Instead he establishes a mood or expresses a feeling. He doesn't so much want his audience to act or to understand as he wants them to feel—to feel hope, thanksgiving, or renewed dedication. But in most of our talks we are asked to assume the role of lawyer, rather than that of a teacher or preacher. We are invited to urge passage of a bond proposal, speak in behalf of a candidate, or plead for a new traffic light at a community meeting.

The Advocate Speech

For Advocate talk, I developed some twenty-five years ago the EASE formula, which can be used, for example, by volunteer speakers in urging United Fund donations. Still today former students, seminar enrollers, or readers of *Instant Eloquence or Roles Speakers Play* will come up to me and say, "EASE—I still remember it—Exemplify, Amplify, Specify, Electrify."

It is an EASE-y formula that helps one to organize quickly one's thoughts for the short Advocate talk that urges a specific solution to a problem. Every Advocate talk is broken down that way: explaining the problem and dealing with the solution.

EXEMPLIFY

The first step is to *exemplify* the problem. That means relating a case story, an illustrative anecdote, or personal experience that relates or exemplifies the problem.

In Advocate talk plunge right in with the recitation of a story. If you are urging in your talk a fair share contribution for the United Fund Drive, you might tell about the black youth who was burned in a fire.

> A year ago a tall black youth in St. Joseph's High School had the potential of being a basketball star. His prowess could be his ticket out of the ghetto to which he

163

was born. Yet in the middle of his junior year a fire swept over his home. Luckily none of his family did die. He survived, but it looked as if his basketball playing days were over because of the severe burns he had sustained.

Last week, though, he not only scored the most points, but the winning basket for his team. Because of the treatment provided by the Burn Center supported by your United Fund, he is on the road to being a winner.

It sounds like a soap opera, doesn't it ? Good. That is exactly what grabs the audience's attention—a case example about a real person. Soap Operas are popular because listeners identify vicariously with the trials and tribulations of the characters. They do even more when relate real life situations.

Or let's suppose you are pleading for a new traffic light to be installed in your suburban township. Call the police and find out what serious accidents have taken place at the dangerous intersection. If someone was killed, lead off with that account, detailing the cause of the accident as well as the background of the deceased. Imagine that you are the lawyer representing him in a death action. Every such tragedy has the elements of a story that will win sympathy and arouse interest.

In 1965 I spoke across Pennsylvania on behalf of the Bar Association for the Presidential Disability Amendment. I took the audience back to August 1882 when President James Garfield was felled by an assassin's bullet while heading for a train to return to Williams College for his twenty-fifth reunion. For thirty-eight days, as the stricken President lay in a coma, the decision-making capability of the Executive Branch was also paralyzed. I then asked them to reflect on how vulnerable our country would have been if Kennedy, whose assassination was a recent memory, had lingered on in a similar coma.

AMPLIFY

When you have exemplified the problem, you can then *amplify* on it. Amplification proceeds in either of two ways: more illustrations of the problems or more reasons why the problem has to be rectified. If you can dig up more case examples, tell them this time in a briefer fashion than you did in the opening story.

The Lord High Executioner in Gilbert and Sullivan's *Mikado* says, "I have a little list, I have a little list." If you are outlining the talk on the back of an envelope, you may want to jot down a list either of more examples or more reasons.

> *Exemplify*—Burned basketball player.
> *Amplify*— 1. Marital counseling story.
> 2. Glaucoma test—preventing blindness.
> 3. Blood bank services.

When I *amplified* in the Presidential Disability Amendment speech, I mentioned that if anything happened to then President Lyndon Johnson, who had already suffered one heart attack in 1954, the aged Speaker of the House, John McCormack, would be President, a man little known outside his home city of Boston and little prepared for the rigorous responsibility of the Presidency.

SPECIFY

In a short Advocate talk, when you have exemplified the problem and then amplified on it, you now move to *specifing* the solution.

It was once suggested to William Rogers when he was

Secretary of State that he deliver a talk on the subject of American servicemen who were missing in action in Vietnam. Rogers demurred because he thought that a speech that outlined a problem without a *specific* solution was counterproductive.

In a true Advocate talk there is a solution that must be set out and explained in detail. If it is a talk about the United Fund, the solution is the budget goal, which is broken down into corporate gifts, special gifts, matching gifts, general campaign, etc.

For the talk on the Presidential Disability Amendment, I specified a solution by explaining the proposed amendment and how the various provisions would work. I had to explain how the President's incapacity would be determined and how the new Vice President would be chosen.

ELECTRIFY

After the advocate *specifies* the solution, he must *electrify* the audience to do something about it. A wit wrote, "Benjamin Franklin was born in Boston. He moved to Philadelphia. He married, then he discovered electricity." Well, whatever turned on Ben Franklin, the speaker must turn on the audience. He must galvanize the audience into action.

For a United Fund audience, the speaker asks each one to give his fair share. In another Advocate talk, it might be to write his Congressman to support a specific piece of legislation or perhaps to call his township supervisor about installing a traffic light.

In an Advocate speech, it is important to involve the audience and enlist them. When Tip O'Neill was running for the legislature, he noted that a neighbor was supporting his opponent. He told her, "I mowed your lawn, raked your leaves, shoveled your walk. How could you?" And she answered, "Tip, you never asked me!"

An Advocate speech without any asking is but a lecture. The listeners who could be participants stay spectators. My mother used to be frustrated by the Presbyterian minister whose Sunday sermon boiled down to "be good." She said, "Jamie, he should have asked us to do something specific—like write a condolence letter to a cousin, visit a sick friend in the hospital, or repair a broken friendship."

Well, the reason an Advocate has to electrify an audience is to spur action.

An Advocate has to ask the audience to act. An Advocate's speech that does not ask for audience involvement is a one-way discussion. An audience does not respond to a recitation, but it does respond to a request.

Most of the talks you will deliver in your life will be the Advocate type. You are invited to a service club or church group to urge passage of a bill, to promote an idea, to win approval of a program. For these talks, try the EASE formula. It is so EASE-y the talk almost writes itself.

The Lecture

The second kind of talk is the lecture. To an audience a good Lecturer is more than a teacher—he is a guide, a veteran explorer who takes his hand through new culture, exotic climes, and antique lands. But to be a Lecturer you don't have to be a Baedecker of travel, a Kenneth Clark in culture, or an Edith Hamilton in Greece. You only have to feel that you know more than anyone else in the audience on that subject. You don't have to persuade the audience to your point of view like the Advocate. You only have to persuade them that you are an expert.

You don't do that by tossing at them a lot of scientific terms, bureaucratic acronyms, or insider jargon. The real test for mastery of a subject is the translation of the complex into the simple—making the exotic familiar.

The formula for doing that is *generalize, fragmentize, philosophize.*

GENERALIZE

Imagine yourself on an afternoon helicopter tour of New York City. First, at a distance, you see the whole city spreading before you; then you pass over each of the sections and mark the special landmarks—the Statue of Liberty in the harbor; the Empire State Building, Rockefeller Center, the UN building, and World Trade Center in Manhattan; Shea Stadium in Queens—and finally at dusk you fly away, seeing the profiled skyline. Or, to put it another way, you make your audience stand behind your shoulder—first at a distance to see the whole picture, then up close, and finally at a distance again as you sum up your impressions.

The opening *generalization* can be like an introduction to a book or it may be a catchy description—something that gives the audience an overall view of the whole subject.

My English friend Lord Crathorne gives many talks on art to men's groups and business clubs in this country. To get their attention, he opens:

> Going to an art auction is like going to the stock market. There are the reliable blue-chip paintings of old masters, the paintings of faddish artists like the glamour stocks, and there are the unknowns with long-term

168

potential. Buying paintings is not only a less complex field to master than the stock market, it is also less risky and a safer investment.

FRAGMENTIZE

After you provide an opening insight into your topic, you are then ready for the main meat of the speech. Here is where you *fragmentize*. You know why I used to cut up the meat for my two daughters' dinner? Not because the girls could not do it themselves, but because the big slab of beef is discouraging to a child—it is too much to tackle. But once I carve it up into small pieces, they start on the meat and end up eating it all.

In how-to-do-it speeches on photography or furniture refinishing, you break your speech up into five or six easy steps. In a speech on the stock market, you may divide it up into stocks, bonds, and mutual funds. A book reviewer may talk on the plot, characterizations, and style. You may separate a historical address into time periods or a travelogue into geographical regions.

The secret in organizing your notes for a speech is to break the speech into three or four sections. Once you finish building the structure for one floor of the house, the other two or three are easy because there's a pattern to follow.

TIPS, An Acronym for Organizing Your Speech

A workable formula for bite-size speech portions came to me when I was going to law school and doing some part-time work at the Eisenhower White House. A speech writer there who had been a minister gave me this advice about organizing a speech. "Jamie, here's an acronym to help you organize a speech into easy sections. TIPS," he explained, "stands for *time, importance, place,* and *society.*"

Time

The first word in the formula was *Time*. Most lectures lend themselves to a chronological treatment. For former President Ford's memoir, *A Time to Heal*, on which I was an editorial adviser, it was determined to follow such a chronological course: Youth, Congress, Minority Leader, Vice President, Constitutional Crisis, and President.

A common version of the *Time* format is to examine an issue first from the perspective of its background, then from its present situation, and finally from its future prospects. For example, a speaker on ecology opened his address by sketching the conservation movement from its inception before the turn of the century. Then he analyzed the environmental legislation of the 1970s. He ended by raising the hard questions the next generation would have to deal with in balancing our laws to check pollution against the rising demands for new sources of power.

Importance

The second method of dividing up your speech is scaling to the degree of *importance*. Henry Kissinger, from his position on the National Security Council, used to outline various options on how to deal with world crises. High-risk recommendations such as military force, which offered the surest means of combating the problem, came first, and the safest and most ineffectual courses of action, such as petitions to the United Nations, came last.

Place

Most lectures or informational talks lend themselves easily to being broken down either chronologically by *time* or geographically by *place*.

A member of the National Security Council gave a talk on Africa and broke it down to Arab Africa, then countries formerly colonized by Britain, and finally countries formerly colonized by the French.

We sectionalize the country into the Sun Belt and the Frost Belt. We break up the world into the haves and the have-nots, or into the East, the West, and the Third World.

Society

Society lets you organize a speech along the lines of rural, suburban, and urban; or according to economic layers in society: the unskilled and the unemployed; the skilled and the white-collor workers; and the affluent upper middle class. When we discuss issues in today's society, we become sociologists who categorize people *socially.*

When we differentiate people by religious or racial groups we are *socially* categorizing. We are *socially* separating when we rank workers by the income they earn or the occupations they practice.

PHILOSOPHIZE

After you *fragmentize* a lecture into parts, you then have to put it back together by *philosophizing*.

The *philosophizing* is really summarizing with a moral. You have to communicate the insights that you have learned from your vocation and avocation. "History is philosophy," said Thucydides, "learned from experience."

And that is what you do in your closing of a lecture. You draw out a philosophy from your impressions or insights.

In closing his talk on art auctions, Lord Crathrone *philosophized* by saying:

> I began by saying going to an art auction is like going to the stock market. Well, it's a lot more than that. It's bidding for a piece of yourself, your mind, or an experience you felt. You are providing for the future a reflection of a mood or experience from which you can learn and feel the rest of your life.

Think of a lecture in these terms: you look at the broad picture by *generalizing*, you break it up by *fragmentizing* and then you put it back together again by *philosophizing*.

The Commemorative Speech

The greatest orations in history were Commemorative—or dedicative—the Gettysburg Address and Pericles' Funeral Oration to the Athenians. In my own career of more than a thousand speeches or talks, the two that moved the audience the most and are best remembered were a eulogy of John Kennedy in the Pennsylvania House of Representatives and a memorial address in honor of Sir Winston Churchill. A major key to the enduring popularity of President Ronald Reagan is his ability to express the nation's mood in his Commemorative talks at Normandy and at the death of the astronauts. Why are the Commemorative speeches better remembered than Advocacy talks or Lectures?

Well, for one thing, a Commemorative speech is a ceremony or a rite. We remember the time they presented a gold watch to Joe for thirty years' service long after a travelogue on Norway is forgotten. We remember the day they dedicated the hospital wing long after some speech arguing for the new tax bill. The hot issue of ten or even five years ago has burned out and the cold ashes scattered. Yet certain ceremonies illuminate the past and bring dimension to our memories: "That was the year Bill was installed as Rotary president," or "It was just about this time last year the company had the retirement dinner for Bob." That is a good reason audiences are likely to remember Commemorative occasions more than others.

The problem, though, with many commemorators is that they do nothing to arouse feelings. By just going through the motions, they don't stir the emotions.

A good way to sort out your feelings is to recall an incident or experience that epitomizes your thoughts. After all, to Commemorate means to call to remembrance—nothing is more sentimental than some nostalgic note of the past. Thomas Wolfe's title may claim *You Can't Go Home Again*, but we sure do try to relive those days when everything seemed clearer and simpler.

So the first rule for a Commemorative speech is to evoke a memory. That's easy to keep in mind because the word "commemorate" has the core of memory within it. When you have to deliver a Commemorative address—whether it be some short remarks on Veterans Day or when pinning on an Eagle Scout badge—think of some incident. Perhaps it was a battlefield situation in World War II, Korea, or Vietnam, or maybe it was something your old scoutmaster taught you as a boy. Retell the experience and then the impressions it made and the lessons it taught. A Commemorative speech should be impressionistic.

In a way, speeches are like paintings. The bold lines of a modern abstraction are like those of an Advocacy

173

speech—the simplistic and dramatic presentation of an idea. The Lecture, on the other hand, is more like illustrative realism—perhaps the detailed picture of an Andrew Wyeth, telling you something about a field or a farm girl. But the Commemorative speech is more like an impressionist painting—a picture with warm colors and texture capturing a mood or a moment.

One of my favorite mystery writers, the late Ross MacDonald, has his detective Lew Archer say, "The painter makes objects out of events, the poet makes words out of events." Or, to put it another way, the Preacher or Commemorator paints for the audience a word picture of a certain memory or even the experience. He gets the audience to share with him the impression of that memory.

Again, you have the Commemorative technique—recreate the memory and then distill the message from that memory.

Robert Burns writes:

> *And many a message from the skies,*
> *That something in us never dies.*

Well, in a memory of a man or milestone, there is a message that will never die. It may be courage or conviction, loyalty or love, service or sacrifice, or a combination of these qualities.

It may be the courage of a George Washington, the compassion of an Abraham Lincoln, or the intellectual curiosity of a Theodore Roosevelt.

Judge Learned Hand once wrote: "A man's life, like a piece of tapestry, is made up of many strands which interwoven is a pattern." Sometimes the memory of a man's life offers a combination of qualities that constitute the message.

What's the lesson to be learned, the word to be minded, or the principle to apply? That's the message.

The Commemorator speech begins with the memory, searches for a message, and closes with a mission. In a Commemorative speech, mission is the sense of duty we owe the fallen. Lincoln said in the Gettysburg Address:

> That from these honored dead we take increased devotion to that cause for which they gave the last full measure of devotion; that we here highly resolve that these dead shall not have died in vain; that this nation, under God, shall have a new birth of freedom, and that government of the people, by the people, and for the people shall not perish from the earth.

What does the present generation owe the past? What can the youth owe their forefathers? What do the rest of us owe our heroes? Whatever the duty, that is the mission: to prevent future wars, to keep the democratic process clean, to seek a cure for the diseased or education for the illiterate. The mission takes an abstraction like duty and translates it into an agenda.

Memory, message, mission, that is the formula for the Commemorative talk honoring a man or a milestone.

Chapter 20

Don't Be Afraid
to Be Different

Some years ago the president of a major insurance company sent me the commencement address he was going to deliver to a Catholic university and said, "Jamie, tell me what you think of it. I think it pretty much fills the bill but look it over—it may need some touching up in places."

Like so many commencement addresses he had started out saying:

> As I look out at all your young eager faces, I feel a sense of envy—I wish I were your age again—to have my life before me with opportunities to seize and worlds to conquer—to once again feel the hope that only the youth can radiate with their plans for the future and their dreams for tomorrow.
>
> Yet I must tell you in all candor that shadows darken this most critical time of our century. The specter of war threatens world peace and the danger of inflation sops our economy. . . .

I called him back and said, "I think you can go with those first couple of paragraphs but I would add these sentences:

> You know that is no more true today than it was when Plato addressed his students at the Groves of Academe.
>
> In the first place I don't want to go back to that time when I left college—when I couldn't get a job because I didn't have experience and couldn't get experience because I didn't have a job.
>
> And secondly, I don't really want to be twenty again. I was a lot more mixed up then than I am now. I didn't really like myself at that age. My insecurities were never greater and my inadequacies loomed out of proportion. At my age today I not only have made peace with myself, but I also have begun to cherish some of my faults as idiosyncrasies expressive of my unique personality.
>
> And so far as this being the most critical time of our century, I question that. Actually 1914 or 1939 in Europe was a darker time—so were the Depression years in our country. Why, I can remember back to my own graduation year in the late 1950s when our commencement speaker spoke of the Soviets' launching of Sputnik as heralding the "most critical time of our century." There is a certain egocentricism in assuming your age is the most critical in world's history. . . .

The Cliché-Reversal

The insurance president followed my suggestion and won a rousing reception from the student body for his witty puncturing of prosperity. I call this technique *cliché reversal*.

Many people think that if they say the same thing as

everyone else it must be the right thing to say. Actually what is trite is not necessarily right, and it is bound to be dull—so dull that the audience tunes out as soon as they begin to hear the same old tune.

Joseph Alsop once wrote that Washington columnists are like birds on a telephone wire. Once one flies off, soon the others follow one by one. In the 1986 Congressional campaign, one writer opined that it was the dirtiest campaign season he had ever witnessed, and soon all the other columnists residing on the Washington beltway began to sound the same theme.

I waited in vain for one writer to report that the year was certainly no worse and probably a lot cleaner than a lot of campaigns in the past when they called Lincoln a baboon, Andrew Jackson a murderer, and George Washington a cheat.

A talk stating that the 1986 elections were comparatively clean would be an example of *cliché-reversal*. For a Labor Day talk for William Brock, the then Republican National Chairman, I wrote a speech denouncing big business as "corpocrats," those who piously paraded their faith in free enterprise while lobbying for tariffs, tax shelters, write-offs, and for retaining all the corporate tax deductible perks such as limousines and private jets.

Dick Darman, the undersecretary of Treasury in 1986, denounced "cororacracy" in a similar speech that won wide recognition. He, too, attacked the opposition of big business to the new tax code that eliminated tax shelters and write-offs.

It was an example of *cliché-reversal* because the press expected a Republican spokesman to laud big business, not to lambaste it.

Another speech I drafted employing the *cliché-reversal* was a commencement speech in 1986. Governor Mario

Cuomo of New York had just delivered a much quoted address attacking the generation of students as the "Me" generation, more interested in advancing themselves than the causes of others less fortunate. Again I had the speaker begin by parroting the same cliché but then following with a rhetorical question. "Well, what is wrong with studying hard and preparing oneself for a future career? Escape from one's responsibility in the classroom is no substitute for excellence. . . ."

Another form of the *cliché-reversal* is for the speaker to open by criticizing his audience instead of praising it.

Associations expect speakers to begin by extolling their objectives and accomplishments. But such opening amenities of flattering often serve to reduce the speaker's credibility instead of reinforcing it. Jaded listeners who have heard countless such talks at the convention meetings each year begin to wonder why, if everyone is for them, they are having such a hard time translating some of their agenda into legislative action.

Even speakers who do point out some differences they have with their host organization's policies and objectives begin by praising them. It has the same effect as the acquaintance who tells me, "You have a great mind and great imagination, but you lack discipline." Or, "You have great speaking presence, but you should lose fifty pounds." The receiver of such remarks tends to tune out everything before the "but." When the press heard Richard Nixon say, "Of course, Congress has every right to oppose but . . ," they wrote on what he said after the conjunction.

Martin Luther King, when he addressed business groups, would open by attacking those businesses located in the middle of the ghetto seemingly insensitive to the racism, poverty, and deprivation surrounding them.

The audience was taken aback. After all, weren't they

paying him a handsome fee to speak to their group? Didn't that show that they weren't racists?

But then Dr. King would follow with a paean to business. "Private enterprise," he would say, "is what made America great. It spanned the continent with railroads, it built the factories that produced for the world, it provided the jobs that gave America the highest standard of living. . . ."

Then he would end by saying, "The dreams of the entrepreneur, the dream of the businessman is the American dream, and we blacks want to share in that dream and live that dream."

The result was a standing ovation. It had the emotional combustion of a mother who spanks her son and then takes him in her arms and hugs him. The opening attack by King made the closing praise by King not only more appreciative but more believable. It made him stand out as a leader instead of one who just parrots what everyone else is saying.

Senator Joseph Biden of Delaware, whose oratory lifted him briefly into the ranks of Presidential contenders, once opened a speech to Philadelphia Democrats by attacking their insensitively to the average worker's fear of crime on the streets and drugs in the schools. He said they had too often adopted fad philosophies of the elite while avoiding concerns of a secure home and a strong country. Then, when the audience was taken aback, he extolled and exhorted them as the heirs of Franklin Roosevelt and John Kennedy. The result was a rousing reception.

Plato wrote about the philosopher-king—the leader who would tell audiences not just what they wanted to hear but what they should hear. The *cliché-reversal* approach turns a speaker into a leader.

John Anderson in 1979 put himself above the pack of

other Presidential aspirants when he spoke to Iowa farm audiences and came out against lifting the embargo of goods to the Soviet Union because of their mission in Afghanistan.

Pete DuPont, the former governor of Delaware, is winning early recognition for his Presidential aspirations by his opposition to increasing farm subsidies in his talks to Iowa groups. Courageous politics is, in the long run, good politics, and what is true for politicians applies equally to speakers. If you say what everyone else is spouting, you are a politician not a statesman; you're a parrot not a lion. If you want national recognition, follow Abraham Lincoln's advice and let the audiences be "touched by the better angels of our nature." Appeal to the audience's patriotism, not their prejudices, to their ideals, not their self-interest.

The Futurist-Flash

Another speech approach of the philosopher-king is what I call *futurist-flash*. In a speech I drafted for a utilities executive, I opened by describing a community where lights, except in the bedroom, would have to be turned off after 10:00 P.M., where one day a week no electrical appliances would be used, where electric stoves could not be used for the noonday needs. And then the speaker stopped and said, "The community I am describing is yours in the year 2020. Or it could be—unless we find new ways like atomic energy to fuel our power plants." An ecologist or environmentalist could begin his talk in a similar way by sketching a community where air-conditioning is limited to the months of July and August, and where drinking water has to be purchased and not drunk from the tap.

Some of the most popular speakers I encounter on the lecture circuit are futurists who sketch out the society of tomorrow. The futurist combines the appeal of the astrologer and the excitement of a science-fiction writer. Yet anyone can be a futurist. All he has to do is to confine himself to his own expertise—be it in finance, food, or foreign policy, and sketch out the future, based on the projections of today. Don't worry; no one is going to come around in 2020 and say that you were wrong in the predictions you gave to the Rotary Club thirty years before.

All you have to do in writing a *futurist-flash* speech is to go to the library and examine trends and then project those trends into the next century. Then describe a society or world shaped by those trends. That is what Churchill did when he talked about the eight-hour day in 1901, the use of a superbomb in 1917, and the energy crisis in 1924.

As Churchill himself said, "I have not always been wrong." His imaginative insights into the future captivated audiences and established him as a leader to be watched and listened to long before they turned to him to be their Prime Minister.

Lord Tennyson writes:

> For I dipt into the future, far as human eye could see,
> Saw the Vision of the world, and all the wonder that would
> be.

And you can fill your listeners with wonder as you dip into the future as a subject for your next talk.

The Parallel-Paradox

Equally fruitful as the future is the past. I call this approach the *parallel-paradox*.

> We see the Senate enacting new controls to check the Executive's foreign policy initiatives. We see a Senate increasingly alarmed by a runaway deficit which neither they nor the Executive can control. We see the problems of assimilating new people who seek the citizenship of our nation.
>
> This was the situation Rome found itself in during the days of the leader Sulla, seventy-five years before Christ.

The role of historian as well as futurist helps the speaker to assume the toga of a philosopher.

Some years ago I wrote for a former Cabinet official.

> The Chief Executive from his window of power sees a society of eroding productivity. He sees his government budget distorted by the demand of costly technological and sophisticated weaponry to reinforce the national security.
>
> He sees the spirit of his people sapped by the rocketing rate of drug dependence—people who could lead constructive lives choosing the chemical release of escape from their dreary life.
>
> He sees those of different religions and different color of skin finding themselves not accepted into the mainstream of life but being relegated to an explosive class of substandard citizens.
>
> This is the way the Soviet Premier must see the world outside the Kremlin window, where alcoholism robs almost a third of his people of a productive life—where discrimination prevents Jews, Mongolians, Uzbeks, Kazaks and other Muslims from holding high office or taking a fuller role in society.

183

Speaking as one who studied the classics as well as history, almost any problem of the present has its parallel in the past. "The historian," wrote the German scholar Friedrich Schlegel, "is a prophet looking backward."

And the speaker with any amount—even the skimpiest of research—can ferret out situations in the past dealing with crime, inflation, environment, or foreign policy, and can sketch out scenarios of yesteryear in such a way that the audience is temporarily gulled into thinking you are describing the present.

The audience is then anxious to know what happened to that ancient society and what are the lessons derived from the experience that applies to ours.

If you want to deliver a memorable address, turn you searchlight to what everyone else is saying and reveal the inconsistencies and inaccuracies. Turn the clichés upside down. But if you, or your boss, are wary of the unorthodox and are hesitant about reversing a cliché, you can still sound like a statesman or philosopher by being a historian recounting the lessons of yesterday or by being a futurist projecting the trends for tomorrow.

Part II

SPECIAL ADVICE
FOR SPECIAL OCCASIONS

Chapter 21

A Packet
of Political Tricks

In what looked like it would be a tough Congressional race, Lyndon Johnson was told by aides that his opponent was gaining ground. Johnson reportedly told his lieutenants, "Spread the story that he fornicates with pigs."

"Is that really true?" asked the aide.

"Hell, no," drawled Johnson, "but I just want to hear him denying it."

The tricks of politicians go at least as far back as the first democracy in Greece. In the days of the Roman Republic, Cicero perfected one of the oldest techniques in his campaign against Cataline. He called it *praeteritio*, the act of omitting or neglecting. I call it "the act of being a clean-sounding dirty politician," or better yet "the *Cicero gambit*."

In the fight against Cataline, Cicero said, "I will not talk

about the charges of corruption against Cataline . . ." or "I
am not going to bring up the allegations of embezzlement
against Cataline. . . ."

He didn't have to bring it up. He already had!

The Cicero Gambit

In 1952, Vice Presidential candidate Richard Nixon was
instructed by Eisenhower's campaign staff to do the hatchet
work while Eisenhower presided over a high-minded cru-
sade. He deftly jabbed at Stevenson's divorce with the
Cicero gambit. "It is wrong for Republicans or anyone to
bring up the matter of Governor Stevenson's divorce. This
campaign will be fought on the Truman Record."

Democrats hit back, charging that a fund provided by
contributors to pay for office expenses was somehow
suspicious. Nixon, in his famous "Checkers" speech, defended the fund and asked all candidates to lay bare their
financial records as he had done. But along the way he
slipped in some Ciceronian punches, saying that he would
not criticize Vice Presidential candidate John Sparkman
for hiring his wife as a secretary or pass judgment on
Adlai Stevenson's own secret fund to compensate employees.

Governor Jimmy Carter in 1976 in his campaign against
Ford exercised the *Cicero gambit* when he pledged, "I will
not bring up the matter of Nixon's pardon and I have instructed my staff not to mention the pardon of Nixon by
President Ford."

In the 1980 campaign, when he was challenged by
Senator Edward Kennedy, Carter piously bound himself
to another promise: "I have asked my staff not to bring
up the incident at Chappaquiddick. Whatever happened

to that poor girl is not a matter to be discussed in this campaign; the real issue is that of leadership at a critical time. . . ."

The *Cicero gambit* allows a candidate to get in some elbow digs while posturing as clean and upright. It can be used in diminishing an opponent's credentials in a proxy fight in a corporation or in a zoning battle in a community. I have heard, in a corporate takeover fight, an advocate piously pledge not to mention the subject of a previous messy marriage, as well as another sanctimoniously state that he would not bring up a previous messy bankruptcy in a zoning hearing.

A lawyer will try to bring in extraneous material against his client's opponent in a courtroom. The judge will rule it out of order and direct the jury to disregard it. Of course the lawyer knows that the judge's warning only calls attention to the charge.

If a candidate in a speech dwells at length on trumped-up scandal, it's called a personal attack and may be resented by fair-minded listeners. But the *Cicero gambit* puts it to the attention of the audience while pledging to avoid personal attack.

When Jimmy Carter elbowed Ford with his Ciceronian mention of the pardon, President Ford's team devised another attack which I have called *adjective assassination*.

Adjective Assassination

Carter, after his nomination in Madison Square Garden, led President Ford by thirty points. Part of this advantage was due to Carter's seeming at that time to be all things to all men. He could be perceived as a liberal to liberals, a moderate to moderates, or even a conservative to conservatives. It was important to identify a vulnerability which even his friends and supporters would concede. We came up with the conclusion that even his supporters considered Carter a little different and perhaps a bit odd. The Jewish community and nonevangelicals thought his born-again Christianity "strange." Social conservatives considered his confession of "lust in his heart" in a *Playboy* interview "strange." Scientists, soldiers, and almost everyone else found his reported sighting of a UFO some years earlier a bit "weird." His personal attack on the character of Lyndon Johnson, the previous Democrat President, struck Texans and other Southwest Democrats as "bizarre."

So we in the Ford campaign house gathered some synonyms from *Roget's Thesaurus* for "strange": "odd," "bizarre," " queer," "peculiar," "weird," "eccentric."

Each day a surrogate for President Ford, perhaps a Cabinet Secretary or a Republican Senator, would label a position or statement by Carter as "strange" or a synonym of "strange."

"That is certainly a *bizarre* explanation of his role in. . . ."

"The Governor has made a *peculiar* choice in an economic adviser. . . ."

"It is a *weird* economic proposal Governor Carter is advancing. . . . "

"The alliance with such a powerful interest group can only be described at the very best as *odd*. . . ."

The phrase *adjective assassination* is a modern term for an old Greek rhetorical ploy that transfers by indirection an attack on a policy or person. An ugly word, if used in a personal attack, might be rejected as below the belt, but it is accepted if applied to a program or position. For example, "It is a *corrupt* program. . . ," "It is an intellectually *dishonest* position. . . ." "It is an *insidious* plan. . . ."

Richard Nixon used a variation of *adjective assassination* when he used the noun "traitor" in a speech against Truman. Note that Nixon did not call Truman an out-and-out traitor, as the former President and others have alleged. Rather he said, "Truman is a traitor to the high principles of the Democratic Party when he. . . ."

Opponents of Nixon characterized him as "tricky," and about Ford they sometimes used the adjective "slow-witted." Even if none of these descriptions were true, political opponents deal not with what is real but what people think might be true—the popular perception.

If a candidate is regarded as slick, you might describe his policies as "devious," his explanations as "duplicitous," his actions as "double-dealing," his intentions as "insincere," his goals as "glib." But if Ford was thought to be slow-witted, you might describe his intentions as "insensitive," his understanding of problems as "ignorant," his declarations as "dumb."

Actually, "stupid" did not truly apply to Ford, who graduated higher at Yale Law School than Cyrus Vance, Carter's Secretary of State. (Ford is the only President to have a graduate degree from an Ivy League School.) "Uncoordinated" should also not have applied to a man who is probably the best-conditioned athlete ever to serve in the White House, yet, an impression of clumsiness was spread by reporters. Accordingly an attack by Carter's team on Ford might have described his policies as "disjointed," explanations as "awkward," proposals as "clumsy." Carter had started out thirty points ahead of Ford but by the time of the election the polls were almost a dead heat.

In 1978 Ella Grasso, the governor of Connecticut, was challenged by Congressman Ron Sarasin. Governor Grasso, who was hardly glamorous, did not look neat or trim or slim. Her administration was called a "mess," her approach to problems "disorganized," her record "disheveled," her fiscal management "sloppy." As a result, Governor Grasso, an overwhelming favorite, was pushed into a defensive posture.

This brings up the third political ploy, which the ancient Greeks as well as current semanticists describe as a *euphemism.*

Using Euphemism

The late Everett Dirksen once illustrated the use of euphemism when he told how a candidate for a state civil service job in Illinois handled a sticky problem when filling out an application form. He was asked how his father died. The problem was that his father was hanged as a convicted horse thief. The applicant looked at the blank space for a while and then wrote, "My father died while participating in a public ceremony when the platform gave way."

In an Orwellian world, *euphemisms* proliferate like Topsy. The CIA describes killing as "terminating with prejudice." The Nazis describe genocide as the "final solution."

Churchill as a young man was attacked in the House of Commons for misrepresenting the government's involvement in certain atrocities during the Boer War. When confronted with the charge, Churchill retorted, "It cannot in the opinion of His Majesty's Government be classified as slavery in the extreme acceptance of the word without some risk of terminological inexactitude." An eleven-syllable euphemism for a nasty monosyllable, "lie."

The invasion into Cambodia is called by Nixon an "incursion." The war in Korea is labeled by Truman a "police action." We would rather characterize income tax fraud as "irregularities in reporting" or financial losses as "deferred profit-sharing."

The *euphemism* is the public relations flack's favorite tool. He thinks he is earning his salary by consulting a *Roget's Thesaurus*. But if a *euphemism* is easy, it is also risky, for it invites irony or sarcasm. To label a stink as an "exotic aroma" is to ask for ridicule. Opponents can pick up a *euphemism* and pound its smooth edges jagged with sarcasm or mockery.

If one was attacking Nixon's use of "incursion," one could draw on history and say, "I guess we should describe what Hitler did on September 1, 1939, as his Polish 'incursion.' "

Or if you want to ridicule "mis-speak"—a Ron Ziegler *euphemism* for "lie"—you might want to say:

> Let us rewrite the Bible. Let us rewrite the New Testament to say Peter "mis-spoke" three times, or, in the Old Testament, let us have it read in the Ten Commandments, "Thou shalt not mis-speak against thy neighbor. . . . "

The Time-Allocation Ploy

A better defense of the disagreeable fact or unpleasant news than the *euphemism* is the *time-allocation ploy*. This is a variation of the *Cicero gambit* applied defensively rather than offensively.

Churchill in 1942 began, "We shall not suppress the news of the recent losses of shipping in the North Atlantic. . . ," but then he went on to discuss in greater detail the military victories in Africa.

Unlike Hitler, Churchill did not censor bad news and risk his credibility with the British people. Yet he did soften the impact by limiting his discussion of the bad news and expanding on the potential of the good. If he made a practice of not omitting the mention of obvious setbacks and defeats, he also did not dwell on them. He dealt with them first and quickly moved away to discuss more positive developments at length.

The *time-allocation ploy* frees the defender from the charge of whitewash or cover-up. Often the catchphrases of the *time-allocation ploy* are, "We cannot mitigate the damage sustained" . . . "We shall not walk away from the fact that the company incurred heavy losses" . . . "We will not glide over the unfortunate news that". . . .

But, of course, just as in the *Cicero gambit*, the speaker *is* "mentioning" even as he says, "I shall not mention,"; in the *time-allocation ploy*, he is "mitigating" as he says he is not "mitigating."

In the aftermath of the Bay of Pigs, Kennedy refused to delegate the responsibility of the aborted invasion to anyone else, but then after taking the blame in one sentence he spent most of his explanatory statement outlining steps the Administration would take to correct certain procedures in the CIA and Pentagon, and in such a way that he implicitly shifted blame by steadfastly refusing to do so.

Mayor Fiorello LaGuardia of New York, in admitting a mistake, opened by saying: "When I make a mistake, I make a real beaut," and then he devoted more time to reporting positive developments on the municipal front.

The Mock-Epic

One classical means of political attack is the *mock-epic*. Sometimes criticism of the *euphemism* is elevated to the form of a *mock-epic*, such as the ironic use of a *euphemism* applied to a familiar literary or historical event. Other times it can be used to deflect picayune potshots or nitpicking.

Franklin Roosevelt turned the Republican attacks on him by countering on one charge:

> These Republicans, not content are they to attack me, my wife Eleanor or my sons Jimmy and Elliot—no, not content with that, they now include my little dog Fala. The Republican fiction writers have alleged that an American destroyer was sent to Alaska to bring back Fala, but I can assure you that Fala with every drop of his Scottish terrier blood resents this base canard.

At the 1960 Republican Convention former Republican Presidential candidate Thomas E. Dewey lambasted the Democratic nominee, John Kennedy, for his recent allusion to many of the other leaders in history who were also young men.

> And then, my friends, he proceeded to compare himself to men such as Thomas Jefferson, James Madison and Alexander Hamilton. The only one he omitted, apparently, was Hannibal and I suppose that was because *he* was known for leading elephants across the Alps.

In his writings Art Buchwald is a great master of the *mock-epic*. His secret in writing a daily humor column is to trivialize the serious and aggrandize the trivial—i.e., dismiss the nuclear bomb as a new children's toy and treat the removal of a Presidential dog as a Cabinet shake-up.

The greatest modern expert of the *mock-epic* technique is Winston Churchill. Churchill mocked the ineffectuality of the League of Nations in 1928.

> St. George would arrive in Cappodocia accompanied not by a horse but by a secretariat. He would be armed

> not with a lance, but with several flexible formulas. He
> would propose a conference with the dragon—a Round
> Table Conference no doubt—that would be more con-
> venient for the dragon's tail. He would make a trade
> agreement with the dragon. He would lend the dragon
> a lot of money of the Cappodocian taxpayers. The
> maiden's release would be referred to Geneva, the
> dragon receiving all his rights meanwhile. Finally St.
> George would be photographed with the dragon.

The word "mock-heroic" implies both satire and an epic scale treatment. The Bible, literature, and history offer a wealth of tales for likening to modern events. But it seems to be a waning, rhetorical ploy. Seldom do you read a historical comparison such as the one Congressman John Randolph in the early nineteenth century employed to denounce the appointment of Richard Rush. "Never were abilities so much below mediocrity been so well rewarded—no, not since Caligula's horse was made Consul."

Today rhetorical resort to the *mock-epic* has declined, either because contemporary politicians are less acquainted with biblical tales, classical myths, Shakespearean lore, or historical legends; or if they are, because they believe that such allusions would escape modern audiences.

Yet, even at the state level of politics, I have heard an underfinanced state legislator liken complaints of an overfinanced opponent to "Goliath lamenting the size of David's slingshot."

A true *mock-epic* demands a fuller treatment than just an acid one-line sally. Listen to another of Churchill's Aesopian burlesques against the disarmament talk in the 1920s:

Once upon a time all the animals in the zoo arranged that they would disarm, and they arranged to have a conference. So the Rhinoceros said, when he opened the proceedings, that the use of teeth was barbarous and horrible and ought to be strictly prohibited by general consent. Horns, which were mainly defensive weapons, would, of course, have to be allowed.

The Buffalo, the stag, the porcupine and even the little hedgehog all said they would vote with the Rhino. But the Lion and the Tiger took a different view. They defended teeth and claws, which they described as honorable weapons of immemorial antiquity. The Panther, the Leopard, the Puma, and the whole tribe of small cats all supported the Lion and the Tiger.

Then the Bear spoke. He proposed that both teeth and horns should be banned and never used again. It would be quite enough if animals were allowed to give each other a good hug when they quarreled. No one would object to that. It was so fraternal and that would be a great step toward peace.

The Slogan-Slash

Churchill was also a master of what I call the *slogan-slash*. As leader of the opposition, he coined a refrain to characterize the Labour Government's misadventures in foreign policy as well as its chief spokesman, the demagogic Welshman, Aneurin Bevan: "They are a trio of misfortune—Abadan, Sudan, and Bevan."

The *slogan-slash* is exactly as it sounds—a derogatory slogan intended to slice away at an opponent's vulnerabilities.

In the 1976 Presidential campaign against Jimmy Carter,

I fashioned for one Republican Senator the *slogan-slash* against the Georgia governor.

> Jimmy Carter goes to Iowa and says, "I'm a farmer." But when he journeys to Cleveland he asserts, "I'm a businessman by background." Yet when he lands in Boston and goes to Cambridge, he calls himself a nuclear physicist. Then recently in San Diego he says, "I was and will always be a Naval Officer."
>
> To people who ponder these variations he has one answer: "Trust me."
>
> In New York City he spoke out for cuts in defense; then weeks later in Seattle Washington he calls for stronger missile defense. To those who consider these contradictions, he says: "Trust me."
>
> In Philadelphia he demands a check on inflation and the rising cost of food. Yet in Omaha, he talks about a fairer price for farmers. When voters wrestle with these contradictions, he answers: "Trust me."
>
> In New York he announces to the Urban League his support for an expanded open housing and an end to segregated living. Yet in Florida, he describes his position as favoring ethnic purity of the neighborhoods.
>
> When asked to explain this inconsistency he tells us: "Trust me" . . .

Those with other examples lead up to a crescendo, ending with the Lincoln maxim, "You can't fool all the people all the time." The *slogan-slash* is a political refrain. Politicians use it often in the hope that the audience will begin mouthing the refrain at the appropriate place.

One of the most famous *slogan-slash* refrains was coined by that political virtuoso Franklin Roosevelt. In 1940 he fashioned this attack for the farmers' ears in the usually Republican Midwest. Exploiting the names of Republican

Minority Leader Joe Martin and the two New York Congressmen Bruce Barton and Hamilton Fish, he would chant, "I still remember the great historic trio that has consistently voted against every measure for the relief of agriculture, "Martin, Barton, and Fish."

In Roosevelt's case the *slogan-slash* was a familiar refrain he would recite once in every speech or several times in the same talk. The result was the same: a battle cry for campaign workers and a memorable phrase for political fun and merriment.

The Newspaper Noun

A final arrow in the quiver of political tricks is what I label the *newspaper noun*. The *newspaper noun* targets not so much the audience for the speech as the reporters representatives covering the speech. In short the speaker is looking for the headline or caption in tomorrow's paper or the quick film clip in the evening news. The *newspaper noun* is often an unusual ear- or eye-catching phrase that crystallizes a problem or a program in a sensational way.

Reagan's alliterative description of the Soviet Union was "the evil empire." Franklin Roosevelt described those who opposed his New Deal programs as "economic royalists." Perhaps he was taking a leaf from his cousin Theodore's book. TR had characterized his big business opposition as "malefactors of great wealth." Both sobriquets caught the imagination and stirred consternation in the popular press.

In recent years a similar phrase that caused the most outcry was Vice President Spiro Agnew's characterization of the eastern college students, whose demonstrations often resulted in violent clashes, as "an effete corps of intellectual snobs." The speech writers hit a nerve in Middle America that surprised Nixon and the White House staff. (Agnew had become a hero to many white ethnics and soon thereafter Nixon directed his Vice President to attack media bias.)

Bill Safire, in an almost tongue-in-cheek parody, coined in a later speech for the Vice President "the nattering nabobs of negativism." In both of the Agnew speeches, unusual words were extracted from the dictionary to get the headlines—e.g., "nabobs" and "effete" (although an adjective).

In declaring war on December 8, 1941, Franklin Roosevelt used the word "infamy" to the same effect. How many times have you heard that in conversation. He could have said with assonance and alliteration: "Yesterday, December 7, 1941—a date that will live in *disgrace. . . .*" But Roosevelt and his speechwriters knew that "infamy," a stronger and more unusual noun, would catch editorial attention.

An unusual word that causes reporters to scramble for their dictionaries is the ideal *newspaper noun*. Harry Truman described those in the Republican 80th Congress who opposed his Fair Deal Program as "snollygosters." (In "snollygoster" Truman perceived, as Churchill once said, that *SN* has a pejorative sound: as "queasy," "queer," "quack"; or "sneaky," "snide," or "sniveling"; "squalid," "squinting," "squealing.") In any case, the word caused writers to devote sidebar stories just on the derivation of the word. One scribe who often overuses this ploy is Bill Buckley. He characterized one liberal critic as "retromingent" (urinating backward).

Unfortunately the ingenious use of esoteric or rustic words as epithets has declined in recent years, making political campaigns as homogenized as the candidates. But a careful search in *Roget's* can glean a raft of rhetorical ripostes that will delight audiences and will gain press attention.

The trick in using a *newspaper noun* is to frame the word or phrase in a simple sentence, where the meaning is clear from the context and where the other words are not Latinate polysyllabics that detract attention from the key word.

Former Secretary of State Alexander Haig might have smothered Roosevelt's "infamy" by saying "In the hours of the dawn previous, on the seventh day of December, there eventuated a milestone never to be effaced for its invidious infamy. . . ."

The *newspaper noun*, like all the other political tricks such as the *Cicero gambit*, the *time-allocation ploy*, and the *slogan-slash*, is a rhetorical tool that should be understood but not used to excess. Americans are suspicious of those politicians who in Britain are sometimes described as "too clever by half."

Chapter 22

How to Run a Meeting

The two highest parliamentary positions in the United States are those of the Speaker of the House and the President Pro Tempore of the Senate. But there is a significant difference in their roles and duties. The Speaker, who is elected to the post, is the chief spokesman for his party's position and the manager of the party's legislative program. The President Pro Tem of the Senate is not elected—he succeeds to the office by virtue of his seniority. He doesn't "lead" but only presides over the Senate (in the absence of the Vice President of the United States).

But if the President Pro Tem acts like a referee, the Speaker is a pilot. The Speaker is a participant, whereas a presider is passive. The former is a leadership position and the latter is not.

Be a Pilot, Not a Pussycat

If you are presiding over a meeting, it is important to understand whether you are a pilot like the Speaker of the House, or an umpire like the President Pro Tem. For example, if you are asked to chair a political debate or preside over a town meeting, your role will be that of a moderator or arbiter. On the other hand, if you are chairing a meeting of an organization by virtue of the fact that you are the president of that organization, then you'd better be a pilot and not a pussycat. A chairman of the board who doesn't pilot a stockholders' meeting may find control of his company pirated. And if the president of the local Jaycees or the business and professional women's group doesn't take charge of the monthly meeting, that officer will see himself or herself run over or run out.

To put it another way, is your presiding role just one of your executive responsibilities, or is it a judicial function lasting only for the duration of the meeting?

Twenty years ago a fellow member of mine in the District of Columbia Young Republicans learned the difference between the two roles and did so the hard way. As first vice president, substituting for the absent president, he found himself chairman of the monthly meeting. Customarily, there was a short business meeting before a guest speaker addressed the organization, but that night the business meeting expanded into a three-hour rambling argument about the quality of the canapes served by the contracted caterer at the reception that had been hosted by the Young Republicans. Disagreements raged over who had responsibility for hiring the caterer—the program chairman or the head of the hospitality committee.

Whatever hopes the personable stockbroker had of succeeding to the presidency of the DCYR were dashed

203

as he allowed the meeting to careen out of control in a crossfire of amendments, motions to table, and moves for "the previous question." This group, which was dominated by political types who worked as congressional aides during the day, made life miserable for the hapless vice president, who had been catapulted to that position mostly because of his smooth appearance and nonabrasive personality.

The Senator who had been invited to speak before the group angrily upbraided the young man for the delay. The unfortunate innocent replied, "How am I responsible? I am only the referee."

The chairman of a meeting has to be more than a referee—he should be a railroader. He has to be an engineer who makes sure that no surprises will crop up that could lead to disasters. He has to control the agenda in such a way so that only those items that can be quickly dispatched are brought up.

This incident, however, had its positive value, since it led to the formation of a workshop in which to learn parliamentary rules. Our teacher was an ex-member of the Communist Party who, in her instruction, revealed some of the parliamentary tricks that cadres of Communists would pull in order to subvert the wishes of the majority and gain control of an organization.

How to Manipulate a Quorum

One way was to manipulate the quorum, which is the number required for the conducting of business. A quorum may be a majority or a percentage of the membership. (Sometimes there is even a set number.) If a quorum is reached at the beginning of the meeting, it is valid for the duration of the meeting, regardless of how many leave in the interim. The Communists would delay the proceedings until 3 A.M., when their group made up the majority of those who had stayed, and then they would pass whatever item they wanted to.

How to Manipulate the Agenda

Another ploy was to flood the agenda with trivia. Usually, to place a new item of business on the agenda required a written request before the meeting. So, to create havoc, they would overwhelm the chairman with a spate of letters asking for consideration on all kinds of contrived issues. With a weak chairman at the helm, they could successfully sneak across one of their pet projects in the welter of confusion.

How to Stall a Majority Vote

When a majority vote was likely to eliminate one of their favorite programs, a fellow Communist would rise on a "matter of personal privilege"—a procedure that would force all proceedings to stop. This motion, which has precedence over all other motions, is one way to interrupt the chairman and stall any other actions on the floor. (Contrary to its sound, it is not a reply to a personal attack but is instead an emergency procedure to be used in case of fire, faulty lights, or some other external problem.) Actually, the personal privilege raised by the Communist infiltrator was never without basis, since his associates had sabotaged the lighting or heating system to make the claim justifiable.

205

Packing the Executive Board

The other tactic a minority faction employs to gain power is to load the executive board with their own members. Those who seek out dirty committee work that no one else wants can maneuver themselves onto the board. To such a board, whose members usually sit by appointment rather than by election, is delegated the day-by-day authority of handling club business. Once the Communists controlled it, they would schedule their meetings at inconvenient times and inaccessible places so that their small minority could dominate the votes despite the opposition of most of the members.

How to Outmaneuver Dissidents
and Run a Good Meeting

To combat all those parliamentary devices and gimmicks successfully, you don't have to memorize Robert's Rules of Order. In fact, it might be better if you never looked at it. That was the best advice the former member of the Communist Party gave us.

"If you want to know how to run a meeting," this woman told us, "run it—that is manage the agenda, control the discussion, direct the vote."

She drilled us to "operate under the assumption that you have a majority vote behind you—after all, you were elected by a majority—and don't let a group of dissidents frustrate the majority by getting away with a show of parliamentary tricks."

If you are elected to chair meetings, keep in mind that the majority does not come to watch clubhouse lawyers duel or to hear compulsive talkers vent their egos. It comes in order to do business, and it hopes to accomplish that task in a reasonable amount of time.

The majority has elected you to "run" the meeting. It has delegated that executive responsibility to you. It has chosen you as the best person for the job. If you do that job well, you will have the backing and gratitude of the majority every time.

Five Guidelines for a Crisp Meeting

1. AN AGENDA

Write out beforehand what you think your club or association has to decide on and send the list to the membership along with the meeting announcement. (Occasionally some may write in additional items to be included.)

2. TELEPHONE CAUCUS

Call leading and influential members of the club and sound out their reactions to the major items on the agenda. The aim will be to develop a strong nucleus committed to particular solutions. It may help to draft the actual wording of the motion and to select the proposer, seconder, and speakers on the issue. A few dissidents may accuse you of "railroading," but the majority will appreciate your elimination of trivial details and the time-wasting argumentation over them. A successful leader cultivates a cadre of those who are the ablest and most active in the organization.

3. RULE THE CLUBHOUSE LAWYER OUT OF ORDER

Rule "out of order" those would-be politicians who try during the meeting to concoct diversions to the mail business on the agenda. "John, this is not an exercise testing your knowledge of parliamentary procedure. If you have a complaint, put it in a letter, and I will place it on the agenda for the next meeting." You have every legitimate right to cut off people who ramble on and try to beat an issue to death. Just make sure you do it courteously. "Tom, I'm going to rule you out of order. Time doesn't permit an endless discussion of the issue."

4. Announce Beforehand a Time Limit

Tell the group when you are first elected that you intend to conclude these meetings within two hours (or one and one half) no matter what—out of consideration for their busy schedules. This enforces your authority to cut short speeches and time-wasting maneuvers. Constant reminder of the clock helps to expedite the business of the meeting.

5. Don't Be a Referee—Be a Railroader

Above all, remember that the basic premise behind Robert's Rules of Order, or any other code of parliamentary procedure, is that if someone objects to any ruling of the chair, he can always appeal it. So if a person doesn't like the way you are running a meeting, put the burden on him to interrupt you and prove that the majority agrees with him. Keep in mind that the typical member resents the abstractionist who extends the length of the meeting. You will find that if you forget Robert's Rules of Order and use your common sense, very few rulings will be overruled— and, what's more, you will look like a leader.

Chapter 23

TV Tips

In 1977 I was promoting a book around the country entitle *How to Get Invited to the White House*. On one fall Wednesday morning, I was scheduled to appear on a St. Louis TV interview show at 9:00 A.M. At 8:30 A.M. when I entered the studio, I was met by an apologetic producer who said, "Mr. Humes, I'm afraid we're going to have to cut you to a brief mention of your book—if that. We are fortunate to have Elliott Richardson. He has agreed to be interviewed. Ambassador Richardson is speaking to the St. Louis World Affairs Council, and we are so happy that he has agreed to stop by."

I replied, "Not at all. Elliott is a friend of mine and a man for whom I have unbounded admiration. I suppose Ambassador Richardson is talking on 'Law of the Seas.' "

"Yes," she answered.

Well, I knew Elliott, and I have heard him speak. While he can be very witty in private at a dinner or over drinks, a microphone or camera in front of him turns one of his talks into a pontifical drone. Here is a brilliant man who has been Secretary of just about every Department in the Cabinet, yet when he opens his mouth, his speeches are sometimes so soporific that his addresses are most appreciated by insomniacs.

So I said to the producer, "I will stand by just in case, and I will bet that, after about five minutes, you will hear a gigantic click, which will indicate a massive switch of channels in the St. Louis TV area. You just put up your right thumb, and I'll sit down with you."

In fact, only about three minutes had elapsed, and Elliott Richardson in his "Laws of the Seas" presentation was only up to John Grotius and the sixteenth century when she waved me in saying, "Well, that is very interesting, Ambassador, and I'm sure James Humes who served with you in Washington has some interesting comments to add on the Washington scene. You know he was a speech writer for both President Nixon and President Ford."

Well, the moral of this story is that you can do everything technically right for television and still fail to get your message across.

For the television camera, Elliott Richardson is ideal. He looks like Clark Kent in Brooks Brothers clothes instead of a cape. In contrast to my beefy appearance and round face, he has the angular planes and square jaw of a leader. He was also wearing the right clothes for television—a navy blue suit with a blue shirt and a conservative red and white regimental striped tie. (Navy blue, not black, is the best for men, while royal blue or pastel are the best for women.) He wore long black stockings (no distracting bit of flesh between the knees and ankles). Similarly his oxford button-down blue shirt was not sleeveless (more distraction if the flesh of the lower arm shows) and no cuff links (gaudy jewelry picks up reflections from the camera as do loud prints on women's dresses).

In other words, the ambassador was dressed with the conservative authority appropriate to a guest interviewee. Perhaps he did not smile enough, but he did look his interviewer squarely in the eye and did not keep his hands folded, which tends to make an interviewer more rigid because the expressiveness of hands is never used.

His problem was not so much that his appearance was stiff but rather that his presentation was. Television, and that includes the newscasts as well as the interview shows, is entertainment. Anchormen, anchorwomen, and television hosts and hostesses live and die by their ratings. A noncelebrity who is entertaining does more for the ratings than a celebrity.

That does not mean that you are expected to tell jokes. You have been invited to appear on the program because you have recently done something newsworthy or because you have expertise in a newsworthy subject. The show producer has asked you to be a guest on the show because you, or the subject you are going to talk on, are "hot" news.

It is the interviewer's task to draw from his or her guest a startling admission or damaging quote. You can expect that his staff will have produced for him clips from every newspaper story or magazine article. He or his staff will have examined the various steps in your career. From that he has an idea in what direction he wants the interview to lead.

You might think that your first priority in preparing for an interview is to figure out the questions he will ask. But, no, your first priority is to establish the message you want to leave with the audience. In drafting a speech, you should, as Churchill suggested, write out the single most important thing you want to communicate and then figure the many different ways you could say it. Think up some clever zinger lines that express your message, quote some authorities that reinforce your theme, narrate some anecdote that graphically conveys your point.

When you have done that, then you can game-plan the interviewer's possible questions. The reason you don't ferret out his possible queries initially is that you want to be sure you have a game plan of your own before you think of your responses to his questions. In other words, you want him to play your game and not the other way around.

In tennis, if your only goal is to return your opponent's volleys safely, you will soon lose control of the game. You want to put your own spin on his volleys.

For example, during the time when Irangate was a hot topic, I was speaking to a Madison, Wisconsin, audience on "Confessions of a White House Ghost." At an interview before the speech, the first question posed to me was, "Mr. Humes, you have been in Washington. What do you think went wrong?" I did not want to be sidetracked into a discussion where I knew little beyond what I had read in the papers. So I answered, "The last thing I was consulted on concerning Iran was a toast I wrote for President Nixon in 1969 to the Shah. I wrote, 'Ecbatana was the capital of Media, the forerunner of Persia or Iran, and Ecbatana means in Farsi a meeting place where people of different faiths and religions meet to discuss peace.' You see a speech writer's job is finding new and interesting and quotable ways to express old clichés. . . ."

Just remember there is no one who monitors the interview and points out afterward that you did not directly answer the interviewer's questions. Kennedy in 1960 and Carter in 1976 in their Presidential debates did not answer the questions directly, but they did manage to convey repeatedly their themes: "Let's get this country moving again" and "We want a government as good as its people."

What is the message you want to convey? For the interview, you have researched for that fascinating case story, and you have coined the zinger quotation that will be remembered. To each question you want to see how you can wedge that quotation or anecdote into your answer. If you do, the next question will often follow up on your answer, and you have the interviewer playing in your territory.

Sometimes the question does not so much lead you into a difficult area as lead you nowhere. When I wrote *How to Get Invited to the White House and 100 Other Glamorous Gambits, Clever Ploys, and Foxy Face-Savers*, I was asked by the interviewer how long it took me to write the book. (How involved can an answer be to how long it takes one to write a book?) I answered, "The book itself actually took me a short time. The real problem was doing it in secrecy, because my editor thought the ideas were so good that some celebrity would steal them and write them under a book of his own."

A friend of mine in answering the same question on a book about politics said, "The real problem was not writing it, but the telephone threats I had warning me not to publish it."

Remember, television is entertainment. If you are interesting and fascinating, the interviewer will let you guide the course of discussion. But if you are a dull and plodding pontificator, the interviewer will push you into subjects that are controversial with more audience appeal.

When you prepare for your interview, choose the most arresting statistic, the most sensational example, the most amusing anecdote, or the most poignant personal experience that can be employed to advance your argument, prove your point, or convey your message.

For television interviews, just remember your ABCs.

A. for *appearance*—dress conservatively and look directly at your questioner.

B. for *brevity*—TV interviews usually last only for three or five minutes. You must spend that time conveying your points and not answering his questions at length. Don't be long-winded and keep your anecdotes brief.

C. for *communication*—boil down your message to one sentence. Get it across quickly even if you have to wedge it awkwardly into one of his questions. Use only those quotations or statistics that reinforce that message.

Index

Index